The
Theatre Lover's
Cookbook

The
Theatre Lover's
Cookbook

Recipes from 60 Favorite Plays

by Mollie Ann Meserve
and Walter J. Meserve

FEEDBACK THEATREBOOKS FT/PP & PROSPERO PRESS

Feedback Theatrebooks & Prospero Press
305 Madison Avenue, Suite 1146
New York, NY 10165

Order Department
P.O. Box 174, Naskeag Point Road
Brooklin, ME 04616-0174

ISBN   0-937657-11-5

Table of Contents

INTRODUCTION

This book is based on the assumption that those who care about what they see and hear also care about what they taste, that those who seek a good evening's entertainment are also interested in a good dinner, that those who are particular and discriminating in one area of their lives apply the same standards to other areas--in short, that those who love the theatre also love good food.

Many years of studying the theatre have convinced us that good food for the soul is as necessary to one's emotional well-being as proper nutrition is to excellent physical health. And we are happy to observe that food and the theatre are often linked--in the plays themselves!

Of the countless plays in which food is cooked, served and discussed, we have chosen sixty of our favorites (in a few instances, we've cheated a bit and created a recipe that we think is appropriate for a play that does not actually have that food in it), and we notice that most of these plays are also popular with audiences around the world. Who can forget *Arsenic and Old Lace,* for example, or *Harvey,* or *The Man Who Came to Dinner* ? What high school drama club has not produced *Our Town*? What community theatre has not delighted audiences with *Blithe Spirit* ? And those showgoers who didn't make it to New York to see *The King and I* or *South Pacific* o n Broadway surely know them from road shows and their popular movie adaptations.

Because so many of our favorite plays are frequently produced, we believe you will find many opportunities to use this book--and in a variety of ways.   Perhaps you belong to a readers theatre group (similar to the one we loved in Bloomington,

Indiana) which meets in members' homes just for the pleasure of reading plays. How better to celebrate a reading of *The Member of the Wedding* than with a batch of Berenice's Cookie Man Cookies for refreshment? Or maybe you plan to take your best girl or guy to the theatre for a birthday treat. Why not follow the show with a serving of Birthday Party Cake, appropriate to so many of the plays we enjoy? If you meet friends at the theatre, bring them home for a late-night bowl of Minestrone with Parmesan Cheese, or Ham and Avocado Sandwiches. If you plan to attend a matinee, invite your party to a Special Pre-Theatre Luncheon. (We recently served De Lawd's Rejects Fish Sandwiches--minus the muffins--as an appetizer, followed by Jenny's Spaghetti with Fresh Basil Sauce and Hysterical Mousse Pie.) A dinner celebrating an evening at the theatre might begin with Salad 13 Plus, progress to Chicken of Champions and conclude with Lizzie's Lemon Cake or Nellie's Normal Blueberry Pie.

However you use *The Theatre Lover's Cookbook,* we hope you will find pleasure in reading our brief comments on the plays and in preparing, serving and eating our delicacies.

Each recipe in this book has been developed and proven in our kitchens (in Maine and New York City). Although the dishes range in complexity from Grandmother's Ravioli (from *The Subject Was Roses*) and Beef Bourgignon de Bergerac (from *Cyrano de Bergerac*) to Walter's Scrambled Eggs (from *A Raisin in the Sun*) and Boiled Onions (from *East Lynne*), we think all the recipes are clear and easy to follow. You should be able to find most of the required ingredients in a well stocked super-market, although an occasional trip to a specialty shop may be necessary.

We have created the recipes with everyone's good health in mind and, whenever possible, have included low-fat substitutes in the lists of the ingredients. Almost every recipe calling for butter, for example, lists margarine as an alternative. Egg substitute is listed, whenever viable, along with eggs. Low-fat sour cream or non-fat sour cream substitute often appears. And we seldom specify an exact amount of salt. We heartily approve of fresh fruits, vegetables and herbs, and our recipes call for them whenever appropriate. Finally, we suggest that consumption of red meats, deep fried dishes and rich desserts be limited to special occasions.

In determining preparation times for the recipes, we have included the assembling of ingredients and activities such as peeling, chopping and mincing, plus those steps that do not require your constant attention (baking, simmering and chilling, for example). The preparation time begins when you enter the kitchen to work on the recipe and ends when you serve the dish.

The recipes in this book have given us a great deal of pleasure--as have the plays themselves--and we hope they will do the same for you.

W.J.M.
M.A.M.

+-X÷+-X÷+-X÷+-X÷+-X÷+-X÷+-X+-X÷+-

THE ADDING MACHINE
By Elmer L. Rice
(1923)

Always preaching individual freedom from tyranny, Rice (Reizenstein) was the only American dramatist whose plays were produced in New York both before World War I and after World War II-- from the popular *On Trial* (1914) to *Cue for Passion* (1958). One of the few examples of Expressionism in American drama, *The Adding Machine* is a satire on America's mechanized society, with Mr. Zero as a symbol of the white-collar slave. Called a "waste product," Zero murders his boss and is found guilty by a jury.

Scene 5 finds Zero in a second-rate cemetery, where he meets Shrdlu, who confesses his "sinful nature" and describes a fateful Sunday dinner. The minister was a guest. Shrdlu's mother held the dish with the leg of lamb.

> Shrdlu: She leaned forward, just as she always did, and I could see the gold locket around her neck. It had my picture in it, and one of my baby curls. Well, I raised my knife to carve the leg of lamb-- and instead I cut my mother's throat!

We hope you will choose the carver of your leg of lamb very carefully. In the following recipe, however, we have absolute confidence.

1

SHRDLU'S LEG OF LAMB

For a party of 8.
Preparation time: about $1^1/2$ hours, including roasting.

A 7-8 pound leg of lamb, with the fell (outer
    membrane), most of the fat and the chine (knee
    to hip bone) removed
2-3 cloves garlic, peeled and cut into slivers
1 teaspoon dried thyme
Freshly ground black pepper, to taste
1 tablespoon olive oil
2-3 small onions, cut into quarters or wide slices

For the sauce:
1 tablespoon butter or margarine
1 tablespoon flour
1 cup chicken stock

Preheat the oven to 400° F.

Remove most of the fat from the lamb, leaving a thin layer. Place the lamb, fat side up, in a roasting pan that has been sprayed with non-stick spray. Make several gashes in the fat and insert a sliver of garlic into each. Season the lamb with the thyme and pepper and rub with the olive oil. Place the onions in the pan.

Roast, basting occasionally, about 1 hour, or to 120°-125° F on an instant-reading thermometer, for rare; or 2 hours, to 170° F, for well-done meat.

Remove the lamb from the oven and place on a carving board, cover loosely with foil and let stand 20-30 minutes before carving.

While the lamb stands, make the sauce: In a skillet over medium low heat, blend together the butter or margarine and the flour to make a smooth paste (roux). Remove and discard the fat from the roasting pan. Add the remaining pan drippings to the skillet. Add the stock, raise the heat to moderately high and cook, stirring constantly, until the sauce thickens.

Carve the lamb into thin slices and arrange, along with the onions, on a warm serving platter or individual plates. Drizzle some of the sauce over the slices and serve the remaining sauce in a bowl. (Mint jelly, particularly the kind containing bits of mint leaves, is also very good with the lamb.) Serve the lamb with rice or boiled new potatoes, steamed broccoli and Parker House Rolls (page 20).

AH, WILDERNESS !
By Eugene O'Neill
(1933)

Sean O'Casey, the Irish playwright, wrote of O'Neill: "I've one reproach only to make of him-- that he didn't use his gift for comedy oftener, as shown in *Ah, Wilderness!* " An idealized and nostalgic picture of American family life featuring the coming of age of Richard Miller, a typical O'Neill poet, the play reflects the last of the few happy periods in O'Neill's life.

Act II takes place in the dining room of the Miller home. The family is present, along with Nat's sister Lily and Sid Davis, Essie's brother and Lily's frequently inebriated suiter. The scene revolves around the evening meal and Essie Miller's long-running joke upon her husband.

> Mrs. Miller: Well, I've never told you, because it seemed sort of a sneaking trick, but you know how Nat carries on about not being able to eat bluefish.
> Lily: I know he says there's a certain oil in it that poisons him.
> Mrs. Miller: Poisons him, nothing! He's been eating bluefish for years -- only I tell him each time it's weakfish . . . .
> Lily: Aren't you ashamed, Essie?

Mrs. Miller: Not much, I'm not! I like bluefish!

And so may you!

ESSIE MILLER'S "WEAKFISH"

For a party of 4.
Preparation time: about 15 minutes.

2 whole bluefish*, about $1^1/2$ pounds each, cleaned
    and filleted
1/4 cup butter or margarine, well softened
1 teaspoon anchovy paste
1/4 teaspoon fresh onion juice
1/4 teaspoon fresh lemon juice
Cayenne pepper, to taste
Salt and freshly ground black pepper, to taste
Fresh lemon slices, for garnish

*If someone in your party shares Nat Miller's prejudice, you may substitute mackerel.

Preheat the broiler. When the broiler is hot, apply a generous amount of vegetable shortening to a paper towel and very carefully grease the broiler rack. Place the fillets, skin side down, on the rack and broil, without turning, about 6 minutes.

While the fish broils, combine the butter or margarine, anchovy paste, onion juice, lemon juice and cayenne pepper in a small bowl and blend as thoroughly as possible.

Remove the fish from the broiler to a warm serving platter or individual plates. Spread with the butter mixture, sprinkle with the salt and black pepper and garnish with the lemon slices. Serve the fish, skin side down, with boiled new potatoes, a steamed vegetable and crusty bread or rolls.

In *Ah, Wilderness!*, the bluefish is served with an unidentified soup (recipes for soups are on pages 90, 100 and 185) and boiled lobster, served cold. If you wish to serve boiled lobster (hot or cold) for your *Ah, Wilderness!* celebration, see page 60.

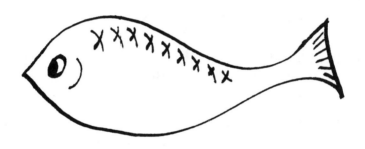

In Act III, Scene 2, the eldest Miller son, Arthur, has just returned from visiting his girlfriend: "We had a corking dinner at the Rands," he boasts, "We had sweetbreads on toast."

> Mrs. Miller: Just like the Rands to put on airs before you! I never could see anything to sweetbreads. Always taste like soap to me. And no real nourishment to them. I wouldn't have the pesky things on my table.

We may agree with Mrs. Miller on bluefish, but she is wrong about sweetbreads. While they do have a strange odor during cooking, they taste nothing like soap and are a wonderful source of protein. We don't know why they are not more popular, as this is our favorite entrée recipe in this book. You too may very well enjoy the "pesky things." Besides, what's wrong with putting on airs once in a while?

WILDERNESS SWEETBREADS

For a party of 4.
Preparation time: about $1^1/2$ hours, including simmering.

$1^3/4$ pounds sweetbreads (fresh or frozen*), with membranes and connective tissue removed
1/4 cup lemon juice
1 teaspoon salt
Melba toast (optional)

For the sauce:
$1^1/2$ cups beef stock
2 celery ribs, with leaves, cut into 1" pieces
2 sprigs fresh parsley
1/4 teaspoon dried savory
1/4 teaspoon dried thyme
1/8 teaspoon ground allspice
1/8 teaspoon ground nutmeg
1/3 cup butter or margarine
2 tablespoons flour
2 teaspoons dry mustard

1/8 teaspoon freshly ground black pepper
1 tablespoon vinegar
1/4 cup coarsely snipped parsley

*Because sweetbreads are not in great demand, your butcher may have only frozen ones. If so, thaw them in the refrigerator and cook soon after thawing is complete.

Rinse the sweetbreads with cold water as soon as possible after purchase. Place in a saucepan and cover with cold water. Add the lemon juice and salt. Cover and bring to a boil over high heat. Immediately reduce heat to simmer and cook 20 minutes. Drain the sweetbreads, plunge into cold water and drain again. (If you are not using the sweetbreads immediately, cool and refrigerate.) Cut the sweetbreads into slices about 1/3" thick and set aside.

Make the sauce: Pour the stock into a saucepan. Add the celery, parsley, savory, thyme, allspice and nutmeg. Bring to a boil over high heat. Immediately reduce heat to simmer, cover and cook 30 minutes. Strain the stock, setting 1 cup of the liquid aside. Heat a large skillet over moderately high heat and add the margarine or butter. Blend in the flour, mustard and pepper. When the mixture is bubbly, add the reserved 1 cup stock and the vinegar and stir until smooth. Bring to a boil, stirring constantly, and cook until thickened. Add the sweetbreads and snipped parsley, turning to coat evenly and heat through.

Bordelaise à la Bordelaise (page 25) is also delicious over sweetbreads, as is the gravy that accompanies Old Lace Pot Roast (page 13), if you substitute 3 tablespoons butter or margarine for the melted fat and add 1/2 cup chopped scallions during the last 2-3 minutes of cooking.

Serve the sweetbreads over melba toast or with wild rice and a creamed vegetable such as spinach, squash or turnip.

≪ ≪

ALL MY SONS
By Arthur Miller
(1947)

This tale of deceit and corruption, so painful to Americans during the 1940's, still touches a raw nerve today. Joe Keller's deception, knowingly selling faulty fighter plane parts to the military during World War II, has wrongfully sent his partner to jail and caused his own son's suicide.

In Act II, the partner's son visits the Kellers. Torn by memories as the family tries to adopt a celebratory pose, Mrs. Keller says: "Listen, to hell with the restaurant. I got a ham in the icebox, and frozen strawberries and avocados. . . ."

Here is our suggestion for a tasty meal made from the strange assortment in the Keller icebox.

HAM AND AVOCADO SANDWICHES

For a party of 6.
Preparation time: about 20 minutes.

12 slices fresh rye bread
Butter or margarine
1^1/2 pound cooked ham, sliced very thin
2 tablespoons mayonnaise
3 cups finely shredded lettuce

1 large ripe tomato, sliced very thin
2 ripe avocados, peeled, pitted and thinly sliced
Fresh lemon juice
Freshly ground black pepper, to taste

Preheat the oven to 350° F.

Lightly spread one side of each slice of bread with butter or margarine. Divide the ham into 6 equal portions and place one portion on the buttered side of 6 slices of the bread. Place these 6 slices of bread in the oven and bake until heated through, about 15 minutes. Remove from the oven. Place the other 6 slices of bread, buttered side up, in the oven and bake about 5 minutes.

While the bread bakes, spread the ham with mayonnaise and top with the lettuce, tomato and avocado. Drizzle a few drops of lemon juice on top of the avocado. Season with pepper. Remove the bread from the oven and top the sandwiches. Cut each sandwich in half diagonally. Serve while the bread is still warm.

For dessert, thaw a package of frozen strawberries and keep refrigerated. Just before serving, spoon the strawberries over vanilla ice cream or orange pound cake (page 46) and top with a dollop of whipped cream.

ARSENIC AND OLD LACE
By Joseph Kesselring
(1941)

This was Kesselring's only successful play, but it was enough. It ran for nearly four years in New York and grossed more than four million dollars. Josephine Hull played Abby Brewster and Boris Karloff her brother Jonathan Brewster.

The action takes place in the Brooklyn home of sisters Abby and Martha, two sweet maiden ladies who take it upon themselves to free lonely old men from the burden of daily living. "For a gallon of elderberry wine," Martha says, "I take one teaspoonful of arsenic, then add a half teaspoonful of strychnine and then just a pinch of cyanide."

Martha's questionable concoction notwithstanding, Abby does make excellent bisquits, which Dr. Harper, the minister, eats to excess just to taste her jam. And Abby's kindness is revealed by the beef broth which she sends to Officer Brophy's wife.

On the evening when Jonathan and Dr. Einstein arrive, Abby and Martha serve a pot roast for dinner. We assure you that the pot roast is superior in all ways and harmful only if you over indulge. If you wish, you may serve an elderberry wine with your meal, but we suggest a store-bought brand and a tamper-proof bottle.

OLD LACE POT ROAST

For a party of 8-10.
Preparation time: $1^1/2$ to 2 hours, including roasting.

2 tablespoons butter or margarine
A 4-4 $^1/2$ pound eye of round, with a thin layer of fat
1/2 teaspoon freshly ground black pepper
4 ounces beef suet

For the gravy:
2 tablespoons flour
2 tablespoons Madiera or port wine
2 cups beef stock
Freshly ground black pepper, to taste

Preheat the oven to 350° F.

Heat a heavy roasting pan over medium heat until very hot and add the butter or margarine. When the butter or margarine is melted and bubbly, sprinkle the roast with the pepper and place, fat side down, in the roasting pan. Increase the heat to high and cook the roast, turning without piercing, until brown on all sides, about 5 minutes. Add the suet to the pan, turn the roast to fat side up, and place the roasting pan in the middle of the oven. Roast 20 minutes. Remove the roast from the oven and drain off and reserve the melted fat. Return the roast to the oven and cook 40 minutes for rare, and another 18-20 minutes for medium rare meat. Drain off any remaining fat. Discard the suet. Transfer the roast to a carving board, cover loosely with foil and let stand 20-30 minutes before carving.

Make the gravy: Return 3 tablespoons of the reserved fat to the roasting pan, sprinkle in the flour and cook on top of the stove, stirring constantly and scraping to loosen any clinging bits, over moderately low heat until lightly browned, about 2-3 minutes. Whisk in the wine and beef stock. Raise heat to high and bring to a boil. Immediately reduce heat and simmer, stirring occasionally, 3 minutes. Stir in any juices which have collected on the carving board. Season with the pepper.

Carve the roast into thin slices, and serve with the gravy, mashed potatoes, a steamed green vegetable and Parker House Rolls (page 20) or bisquits (page 127).

$\$\$\$\$\$\$\$\$\$\$\$\$\$\$\$\$\$$

AWAKE AND SING !
By Clifford Odets
(1935)

"Awake and sing, ye that dwell in the dust" (Isaiah 26: 19). With this play about the agony and near disintegration of the Berger family, where frustration leads to a conclusion that life is "printed on dollar bills," Odets found a very sympathetic audience in Depression-era America. 1935, however, was a great year for Odets, who had four plays on Broadway: *Waiting for Lefty, Till the Day I Die, Awake and Sing !* and *Paradise Lost*.

In Act II, Scene 1, Bessie, the mother, speaks with Uncle Morty, the rich relative:

> Morty: Duck for dinner?
> Bessie: The best Long Island ducks.
> Morty: I like goose.
> Bessie: A duck is just like a goose, only better.

LONG ISLAND DUCK WITH PRUNE SAUCE

For a party of 6.
Preparation time: about $2^1/2$ hours, including roasting.

1 cup large pitted prunes
1 cup port wine
3 apples, peeled, cored and cut into $1^1/2$" chunks

15

1 large onion, peeled and coarsely chopped
2 Long Island ducklings, about 5 pounds each
2 tablespoons butter or margarine
Freshly ground black pepper, to taste

For the sauce:
3 tablespoons butter or margarine
1 cup chicken stock

The day before, place the prunes in a large bowl, cover with the port and let stand at least 12 hours.

Preheat the oven to 450° F.

Drain the prunes, reserving any remaining port. In a large bowl, combine the prunes, apples and onion.

Remove the giblets from each duckling and, if not already removed, the oil sac at the base of the tail. Wash the ducklings, inside and out, in cold water and pat dry with paper towels. Sprinkle the ducklings, inside and out, with the pepper. Place 1/4 of the prune mixture in the cavity of each duckling and truss for roasting (neck and lower cavities closed with skewers, wings and legs tied close to the body). Coat each duckling with 1 tablespoon butter or margarine. Place the ducklings on a rack in a large roasting pan and place in the middle of the oven. Immediately reduce heat to 350° F. Cook, occasionally basting and piercing the breasts with a sharp fork, until the ducklings are tender and golden, about 20 minutes per pound (about 1 hour and 40 minutes).

While the ducklings roast, make the sauce: Melt the remaining 3 tablespoons butter or margarine in a medium saucepan. Add the remaining prune mixture and cook over low heat 15 minutes, stirring occasionally. Add the reserved port and the chicken stock. Raise heat to high and bring the liquid to a boil. Immediately reduce heat to simmer and continue cooking.

When the ducklings are done, remove from the pan to a carving board and let stand. Discard the fat from the roasting pan. Add a bit of the liquid from the prune mixture to the roasting pan, scraping to loosen any bits clinging to the pan. Pour the liquid back into the prune mixture, raise heat to high and bring just to a boil. Reduce heat to simmer and cook about 5-7 minutes. Drain the prune mixture, reserving the liquid (for the sauce) and the solids.

Carve the ducklings and arrange the slices on a warm serving platter. Surround with the prune stuffing and the solids from the sauce. Drizzle the sauce over the slices. Serve with rice and rye bread.

Act III opens in the dining room, with everyone eating hot pastrami sandwiches. As Uncle Morty says: "Everything's hot delicatessen."

HOT PASTRAMI SANDWICHES

For a party of 6.
Preparation time: about 15 minutes.

$1^1/2$ pounds pastrami, sliced very thin
12 slices rye or whole wheat bread
12 slices Swiss or American cheese, sliced very thin
1 large ripe tomato, sliced very thin
1 medium onion, sliced very thin
$1^1/2$ cups very finely shredded lettuce
Mayonnaise and/or prepared mustard or Dijon mustard
Dill pickles, for garnish

Preheat the oven to 350° F.*

Wrap the pastrami in foil, place in the oven and warm until heated through, about 30 minutes. Assemble 6 sandwiches, using each person's choices from the above ingredients. Garnish with the pickles.

*The pastrami can also be heated in the microwave, but do not wrap it in foil -- use waxed paper or butcher's paper instead!

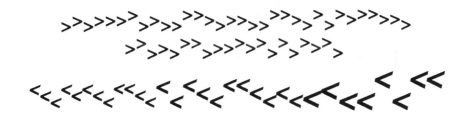

THE BAT
By Mary Roberts Rinehart
and Avery Hopwood
(1920)

A perennial favorite with high school, university and community theatres, this fast-paced melodrama was immediately popular in the United States and England. Like all good murder mysteries, it features misunderstandings and deceptions, as well as a secret room, missing money, disguises, blueprints of the old house, "a black bat" and -- of particular significance -- Parker House Rolls.

With this recipe for Parker House Rolls, you will see how easily they split down the middle when warm, but we suggest that you use this knowledge not to secret a piece of blueprint, but to conceal a small pat of butter.

PARKER HOUSE ROLLS

For a party of 6.
Preparation time: about 1^1/2 hours, including rising, resting and baking.

1 cup milk
1 tablespoon sugar
2 tablespoons butter or margarine
1/2 teaspoon salt
1 package active dry yeast
2 tablespoons warm water
1 egg or 2 ounces egg substitute
2 ^{2}/3 cups pre-sifted, unbleached flour, plus extra
    flour for working the dough
1 tablespoon melted butter or margarine

In a medium saucepan, heat the milk until scalded (when tiny bubbles around the edge of the pan begin to pop). Add the sugar, butter or margarine and salt and stir constantly until dissolved. Remove from heat and allow to cool to lukewarm.

Preheat the oven to 425° F.

Place the water, warmed to 105°-115° F, in a large bowl and sprinkle the yeast over it. Add the milk mixture and beat in the egg or egg substitute. Sift in the flour, a bit at a time, stirring at first and finally using your hands. Use only enough flour to form a dough that can be easily handled. Place the dough in a greased bowl and brush with the butter or margarine. Cover the bowl with a clean dish towel, place in a warm spot and let rise until doubled in bulk.

On a floured surface, roll out the dough to a thickness of 3/4". Cut rounds with a floured bisquit cutter or cookie cutter. Flour the handle of a dinner knife and use this to make a deep crease across the middle of each roll. Push the two sides of the roll up and press together lightly.

Arrange the rolls on a greased baking sheet, place in a warm spot and let rise until they appear to "bloom" or become lighter and fuller. Bake in the middle of the oven about 20 minutes or until golden. Remove from baking sheet immediately and serve hot.

*   *   *   *   *

For a more imaginative way to celebrate your evening out at a performance of *The Bat,* or even a dramatization of Bram Stoker's *Dracula* (1897), you might enjoy a dish of *Winge Chiroptera.*

WINGE CHIROPTERA
("BAT WINGS" IN SAUCE)

For a party of 4-6.
Preparation time: about 1 hour and 40 minutes, including simmering.

3/4 cup ketchup
2 tablespoons vinegar
1 tablespoon Dijon mustard
3 tablespoons Worcestershire sauce
1/4 cup packed brown sugar

1/4 cup liquid from a jar of maraschino cherries
Freshly ground black pepper, to taste
1 tablespoon olive oil
1-2 cloves garlic, peeled and minced
8-10 chicken wings, skin removed
1 small onion, coarsely chopped
1 small green bell pepper, with membranes and
    seeds removed, coarsely chopped
1 small sweet red bell pepper, with membranes and
    seeds removed, coarsely chopped
1/2 cup halved maraschino cherries
1/2 cup drained canned pineapple chunks
1 pound uncooked spinach spaghetti or fettucini
2-3 tablespoons regular prepared mustard
1 tablespoon minced fresh ginger root
1/2 cup sliced scallions
1/4 cup fresh cilantro
Mozzarella cheese, shredded, for topping

In a large bowl, mix the ketchup, vinegar, Dijon
mustard, 1 tablespoon Worcestershire sauce, brown
sugar, cherry liquid and pepper.

Heat a large heavy skillet over medium heat and
add the oil. When the oil is hot, add the garlic and
sauté about 2 minutes. Add the chicken wings,
arranged in a single layer, and cook, turning as
necessary, until lightly browned on all sides. Add
the ketchup mixture, evenly coating the chicken.
Lift each piece of chicken to make sure the sauce
covers the bottom of the skillet. Reduce heat to
simmer and cover. Cook, basting occasionally,
about 30 minutes.

Stir in the onion, bell peppers, cherries and pineapple, coating each addition with sauce. Cover and simmer about 30 minutes.

While the chicken simmers, cook the spinach pasta *al dente,* according to package directions. Drain and set aside.

Stir into the skillet with the chicken the remaining Worcestershire sauce, the regular prepared mustard, ginger root, scallions, and cilantro. Cover and cook about 5 minutes.

Serve Bat Wings over the pasta and top with the cheese. Serve with Parker House Rolls or corn bread.

BEGGAR ON HORSEBACK
By George S. Kaufman and Marc Connelly
(1924)

This experimental comedy satirizing American society proved a surprisingly successful venture on stage. With elaborate exaggeration, Kaufman and Connelly show an artist's romantic revolt against the appealing absurdity of commercial values that attempt to mechanize art. Neil, the hero, must awaken from a dream, one segment of which is set in a restaurant where Neil and Gladys, a wealthy airhead, order a meal from Albert, the waiter.

> Albert: Perhaps Madame would care for some Bordelaise à la Bordelaise, or some Bordelaise à la Bordelaise, or some Bordelaise à la Bordelaise.
> Gladys: Why, yes -- I'd like that!
> Albert: And what will Monsieur have?
> Neil: What is Bordelaise à la Bordelaise?
> Albert: Very nice, sir.
> Neil: Yes, I know, but what is it?
> Albert: It's served in a little round dish-- very nice.
> Neil: Can't I find out what it is?
> Albert: I'll see if anyone knows, sir.

To answer Neil's question, Bordelaise is a sauce; hence, Bordelaise à la Bordelaise is Sauce à la

Sauce. It is excellent on steak, roast or sweetbreads and, although rather complicated to prepare, well worth the effort.

BORDELAISE A` LA BORDELAISE

Makes about $1^1/2$ cups.
Preparation time: about 2 hours, including simmering.

A 4" beef marrow bone
2 sprigs fresh parsley
1/4 teaspoon dried thyme
1 bay leaf
6-8 whole black peppercorns
2 $1/2$ tablespoons unsalted butter or margarine
1/3 cup finely chopped onion
1/3 cup finely chopped carrot
1/3 cup finely chopped celery
3 tablespoons unbleached flour
$1^3/4$ cups hot beef stock
2/3 cup dry white wine
$1^1/2$ tablespoons tomato paste
1/2 cup dry red wine
4-5 black peppercorns, crushed
1/2 teaspoon chopped parsley

Stand the marrow bone on end and split it with a cleaver and carefully remove the marrow. If you don't have a cleaver, ask your butcher to remove the marrow. With a very sharp small knife dipped in water, slice the marrow into 1/4" slices. Rinse the marrow gently under cold running water. In a small saucepan, bring water to a boil over high heat. Drop in the marrow. Immediately remove from heat and let stand until the marrow has softened, about 2 minutes. Drain and set aside.

Tie the parsley, thyme, bay leaf and peppercorns in cheesecloth to make a bouquet garni. Heat a medium saucepan over moderately low heat. Add the butter or margarine. When melted, add the onion, carrot and celery and sauté until softened but not brown, about 10 minutes. Remove from heat and add the flour, blending until the vegetables are evenly coated. Return to heat and cook, stirring frequently, until the flour is golden brown, about 10 minutes. Add the stock, white wine and tomato paste, stirring constantly until blended. Add the bouquet garni. Raise heat to high and bring to a boil. Immediately reduce heat to simmer and cook, stirring occasionally, until the mixture is reduced by half, about 40 minutes.

While the sauce simmers, mix the red wine and crushed peppercorns and cook in a small saucepan over moderately low heat until reduced by 3/4.

Strain the sauce and discard the vegetables and the bouquet garni. Add the red wine mixture to the sauce and simmer about 15 minutes. Gently fold in the marrow and chopped parsley. Serve Bordelaise à la Bordelaise over sweetbreads (page 7), broiled steak (page 157) or roast (page 13), or as a sauce for hamburgers.

THE BIRTHDAY PARTY
By Harold Pinter
(1958)

Some have called Pinter's first full-length play deliberately ambiguous, and the English author has himself appeared purposely vague in discussing his work. The play was first staged on Broadway in 1967 by Alan Schneider.

The main character is Stanley, who lives in a boarding house where he is mothered by the landlady. Two strangers visit Stanley and organize a birthday party for him, although he insists that it is not his birthday. They subject him to a session of menacing questions, accuse him of various acts of misconduct and drive him to a state of severe distraction. The next morning the two strangers take him away.

In honor of the title of this play and with reference to other birthday celebrations in a number of plays--*Crimes of the Heart, The Dining Room, Our Town* and *A Streetcar Named Desire*, to name a few-- we offer an appropriate recipe.

BIRTHDAY PARTY CAKE

For a party! (Makes a 2-layer cake, 8" round).
Preparation time: about 3 hours, including baking
and cooling.

2 $1/2$ cups cake flour
2 cups sugar
1 teaspoon baking powder
1/2 teaspoon baking soda
1/8 teaspoon salt
$1^1/4$ cups low-fat buttermilk
1/2 cup butter or stick margarine, well softened
1 teaspoon vanilla extract
4 egg whites, unbeaten
Zest of 1 orange, finely grated
Juice of 1 orange

For the filling:
2 tablespoons butter or stick margarine, softened
2 tablespoons cream cheese, softened
3/4 cup confectioners sugar
Zest of 1 lemon, grated

For the frosting:
2 egg whites, unbeaten
$1^1/2$ cups confectioners sugar
1/4 teaspoon cream of tartar
1/2 teaspoon almond extract

Preheat the oven to 350° F.

Generously grease and flour 2 8" round cake pans.
In a large bowl, stir together the flour, baking
powder, baking soda and salt. Add the buttermilk,
butter or margarine and vanilla extract. Beat with

an electric mixer on low speed until moistened, about 1 minute. Add the sugar and beat on medium speed about 2 minutes, scraping the sides of the bowl occasionally. Add the egg whites, orange zest and orange juice and beat 2 minutes more. Pour equal amounts into the pans and bake in the middle of the oven until a toothpick inserted in the center comes out clean, about 40-45 minutes. Cool in the pans on wire racks about 10 minutes. Remove from the pans and cool completely before filling and frosting.

Make the frosting: In a medium saucepan, combine the egg whites, confectioners sugar, 5 tablespoons of cold water and the cream of tartar. Stir until well blended. Place the pan over low heat and stir vigorously until the sugar is completely dissolved, about 5 minutes. Remove from heat and pour into a large mixing bowl. Add the almond extract. Beat with an electric mixer on medium speed until the frosting is spreading consistency, about 5 minutes. Cover and refrigerate until the cake has cooled.

Make the filling: In a medium bowl, cream together the cream cheese and butter or margarine. Add the sugar gradually, creaming until the mixture is smooth. Add the lemon zest and blend thoroughly.

When the cake is completely cool, spread the filling over the top of one cake. Top with the other cake. If the frosting has thinned, beat again briefly. Cover the entire cake with the frosting. Serve with ice cream.

BLITHE SPIRIT
By Noel Coward
(1941)

Best known for his pre-World War II witty and sometimes precious comedies, such as *Hay Fever* (1925) and *Private Lives* (1930), Coward continued the English tradition of high comedy in the manner of Congreve, Sheridan and Wilde. During the War, Coward did his best to raise British morale in the face of relentless bombing, and *Blithe Spirit*, a rollicking drawing room comedy, has remained popular, particularly with amateur theatricals.

Act I, Scene 1, ends as a dinner is announced. Madame Arcati, the excessively hystrionic medium who is to solve all problems relating to the spirit world, hopes that there will be no red meat because it sometimes has an "odd effect" on her work. There is meat, which Ruth does not think will be "very red," but we learn nothing more of the meal until Act II, Scene 2.

> Charles: An excellent dinner, Darling--I congratulate you.
> Ruth: The mousse wasn't quite right.
> Charles: It looked a bit hysterical, but it tasted delicious.

In the spirit of the play, Hysterical Mousse is as exciting to prepare as it is delicious to taste.

HYSTERICAL MOUSSE

For a party of 6-8.
Preparation time: about 3 hours and 15 minutes, including chilling.

4 ounces egg substitute
2 eggs, separated
$1^1/3$ cups sugar
1/2 cup plus 1 teaspoon fresh lemon juice
Zest of 2 lemons, grated
2 additional egg whites
1 cup heavy cream

For the garnish:
Whipped cream
Candied lemon peel (optional)
Purée of fresh strawberries or fresh raspberries
    (optional)

In a large heavy saucepan, combine the egg substitute, yolks of 2 eggs, 1 cup sugar, the juice and zest. Stir to dissolve the sugar. Cook over low heat, stirring frequently, until the mixture is thick enough that a spoon leaves a trail, about 50 minutes. Do not boil.

Remove the mixture from heat, place the saucepan in a pan of ice and water to cool, and chill, stirring occasionally, to prevent a skin from forming, about 15 minutes. Transfer the mixture to a large bowl.

In another large bowl whip the cream until peaks form. Returning the bowl containing the lemon mixture to the ice water, stir 1/4 of the cream into the lemon mixture. Gently fold in remaining cream.

In another large bowl, beat the 4 egg whites until foamy. Gradually add the remaining sugar, beating until the whites are stiff but not dry.

Fold the egg whites into the lemon mixture. Transfer the mousse to sherbet glasses and refrigerate until thoroughly chilled, at least 2 hours. To serve, top each serving with a dollop of whipped cream, or candied lemon peel. Or, spoon dollops of chilled mousse onto individual chilled plates and garnish with the strawberry or raspberry purée.

You may also spoon the entire mixture into a baked and chilled crumb pie crust and refrigerate to chill thoroughly before serving as "Hysterical Mousse Pie."

CHAPTER TWO
By Neil Simon
(1977)

Simon's name has long been synonymous with successful light comedy, clever plots and sparkling dialogue. In *Chapter Two*, he combines insight and wit while dealing with the problems of a recently widowed writer facing a new marriage.

Food is not terribly important in the play, but in Act II, Scene 5, Jenny, George's new wife, makes an interesting observation: "I read somewhere you can tell everything about a person by looking inside his refrigerator." Jenny may not be a gourmet cook, but in Act I, Scene 1, she promises to make spaghetti with fresh basil sauce. It is a fine idea, for newlyweds and others.

JENNY'S SPAGHETTI
WITH FRESH BASIL SAUCE

For a party of 6.
Preparation time: about 30 minutes.

3/4 cup extra virgin olive oil
2-3 cloves garlic, peeled and coarsely chopped
6 cups coarsely chopped fresh basil leaves
Salt and freshly ground black pepper, to taste
1 pound uncooked spaghetti
Romano or Parmesan cheese, freshly grated

Heat a large skillet over low heat and add the oil. When the oil is hot, add the garlic and sauté about 2 minutes. Add the basil, salt and pepper. Sauté about 15 minutes.

While the sauce cooks, cook the spaghetti one minute less than called for on package directions and drain. Add the spaghetti to the skillet, increase heat to medium and cook, carefully tossing continuously until the spaghetti is cooked *al dente*, about 1 minute. Test the spaghetti for doneness by tasting. Transfer to a warm serving platter or individual plates. Top with the grated cheese and serve immediately with crusty Italian bread.

In Act II, Scene 5, Jenny perhaps gets closer to her real interest in food.

> Jenny: <u>Everybody</u> wants a chili-burger. Come on, George, a big, greasy, non government-inspected burger dripping with illegal Mexican chili.
>
> George: How many times do I have to tell you, I don't want a goddamn chili hamburger!
>
> Jenny: Chili-<u>burger</u>. The ham is silent. . . .

SILENT HAM CHILI

For a party of 6-8 (or more, if served as a topping for burgers).
Preparation time: $1^1/2$ hours or more, including simmering.

2 tablespoons extra virgin olive oil
1 pound extra lean ground beef
2 large onions, peeled and finely chopped
2-3 large cloves garlic, peeled and minced
2 teaspoons ground toasted cumin seed
1 teaspoon ground toasted coriander seed
1/4 teaspoon (or more) dried red pepper flakes
1 can (28 ounces) crushed tomatoes in tomato purée
1 can (4 ounces) chopped green chilies and their liquid
2 tablespoons tomato paste
2 bay leaves
1 cup dry red wine
1-2 cups cooked and drained kidney beans

Chili powder, to taste
Salt and freshly ground black pepper, to taste
1/4 cup (or more) finely chopped fresh cilantro

For the toppings:
Sharp cheddar cheese, grated
3-4 scallions (green and white parts), chopped
Sour cream or non-fat sour cream substitute

Heat a large skillet over moderately high heat and add the oil. When the oil is hot, add the beef. Immediately reduce heat to medium and sauté about 5 minutes, stirring frequently. Add the onions and garlic and sauté until the onions become translucent. Add the cumin, coriander and red pepper flakes and stir to mix well. Add the tomatoes and their purée, the green chilies and their liquid and the tomato paste. Raise the heat to high and bring to a boil, stirring well. Add the bay leaves. Reduce heat to simmer, cover and cook about 30 minutes. Add the wine, kidney beans and chili powder. Cover and simmer 30 minutes more, or longer, if desired. (The longer the chili cooks, the better it will taste.)

About 10 minutes before serving, skim off any fat that has risen to the surface during cooking, season with salt and pepper and stir in the fresh cilantro.

Serve, as Jenny would, as a sauce for hamburgers, or in heated bowls, topped with the cheese, chopped scallions and a dollop of sour cream and accompanied by warm tortillas.

THE CHERRY ORCHARD
By Anton Chekhov
(1904)

Chekhov's last and most notable play, *The Cherry Orchard* dramatizes the conditions within all societies that are doomed to fade away as old ways of living succumb to the relentless onrush of modernity. It tells of individuals who are incapable of adapting to such movement and of a cherry orchard which is both real and symbolic -- a subject for laughter or for tears, for life can be a comedy for those who think and a tragedy for those who feel.

> Lyuboff Andreyevna, speaking for the aristocracy: Cut it down? My dear man, you must forgive me, but you don't understand anything at all. If there is anything interesting or remarkable in the whole province, it is this cherry orchard of ours.
>
> Lopahin, the practical emerging businessman: The only remarkable thing about the orchard is its great size. It bears fruit only every other year, and even then you don't know what to do with the cherries: nobody buys any.
>
> Gaev: The orchard is mentioned in the "Encyclopedia."

It is clearly an argument that is always with us: the environment versus the economy, tradition versus progress, immediate gratification versus a vision of the future. But, as we ponder, let's do something with the cherries. We suggest something remarkable -- Cherries Jubilee!

CHERRIES JUBILEE

For a party of 4.
Preparation time: about 15 minutes.

A 16 ounce can pitted tart bing cherries
Zest of 1 lemon, grated
1/4 cup plus 3 tablespoons sugar
1/4 teaspoon ground cinnamon
3-4 tablespoons plus 1/2 cup cognac
1 tablespoon cornstarch

Drain the cherries and reserve the liquid. In a medium bowl gently toss the cherries, lemon zest, 1/4 cup sugar, cinnamon and the 3-4 tablespoons cognac. Let stand for a few minutes.

Remove the cherries from bowl and set aside. Add the cornstarch to the remaining contents of the bowl and blend thoroughly. Stir in 3-4 tablespoons of the reserved liquid from the can. Pour the mixture into a chafing dish pan and stir over medium heat until thickened, about 5-6 minutes. Stir in the cherries and heat thoroughly, adding more reserved liquid as needed.

In a small saucepan, warm the remaining 1/2 cup cognac.

To serve, place the chafing dish pan over a flame, sprinkle the cherries with the remaining sugar and add the warm cognac. Heat and, touching carefully with a lighted match, set aflame. When the flame dies down, spoon the cherries over bowls of vanilla ice cream -- or French vanilla ice cream for a special treat!

Ø Ø Ø Ø Ø Ø Ø Ø Ø Ø Ø Ø Ø Ø Ø Ø Ø Ø Ø Ø

THE COMEDY OF ERRORS
By William Shakespeare
(1592-93)

This farce of mistaken identity was adapted to
Elizabethan social conditions from the Latin of
Plautus' *Menaechme.* The confusion surrounding
the meal prepared for Antipholus initiates the
improbable activity.

In Act I, Scene 2, Dromio of Ephesus accosts
Antipholus of Syracuse:

> Return'd so soon! rather approach'd too late!
> The capon burns, the pig falls from the spit;
> The clock hath strucken twelve upon the bell--
> My mistress made it one upon my cheek.
> She is hot because the meat is cold;
> The meat is cold because you came not home;
> You came not home because you have no
> stomach;
> You have no stomach, having broke your fast;
> But we, that know what 'tis to fast and pray,
> Are penitent for your default to-day.

Therefore, burn not this capon for your guests, or
you
May feel upon your cheek one strike or two.

CREAMED CAPON

For a party of 6-8.

Preparation time: about $1^1/2$ hours, including simmering and baking.

1 capon or large roasting chicken (5-6 pounds)
1 teaspoon dried thyme
1 rib celery, with leaves, cut into 2-3 pieces
1 onion, peeled and quartered
1 carrot, cut into 2-3 pieces
2-3 cloves garlic, peeled and halved
1 bay leaf

For the sauce:
4 egg yolks or 4 ounces egg substitute
1 tablespoon butter or margarine, melted
4 teaspoons flour
1 cup light cream or half and half
1 cup low fat sour cream
Salt and freshly ground black pepper, to taste

Remove the giblets from the capon. Wash the capon, inside and out, in cold water and pat dry with paper towels. Sprinkle the thyme into the cavity. Fill a large pot with water and bring to a full boil over high heat. Remove from heat and place the capon in the pot. Add enough water to cover. Return to high heat and bring to a boil. Immediately reduce heat to simmer. Add the celery, onion, carrot, garlic and bay leaf. Cover and cook, skimming off any foam that forms on top, about 1 hour.

While the capon simmers, make the sauce: In a large bowl, cream the egg yolks or egg substitute and the butter or margarine. Add the flour and blend thoroughly. Stir in the cream and sour cream and season with salt and pepper. With an electric mixer or by hand, beat the mixture until light and thoroughly blended.

Pour the mixture into the top of a double boiler and cook, stirring constantly, over, not in, boiling water until thickened. Remove the sauce from heat and hot water and allow to cool, stirring occasionally.

Preheat the oven to 450° F.

Remove the capon from the pot and allow to cool slightly. With a sharp knife, as if you were ready to carve the capon, make cuts in the flesh, across the breasts and between the joints, being careful not to dismember the bird. Place the capon in a greased baking pan. Spread the sauce over the bird, making sure the cuts are filled with sauce.

Place the capon in the lower half of the oven and bake until the sauce is golden, about 30 minutes. Remove from the oven and let stand about 5 minutes before carving.

Serve with new potatoes boiled in their skins, steamed vegetables and whole wheat rolls.

CRIMES OF THE HEART
By Beth Henley
(1981)

A compassion for human frailties coupled with a balanced appreciation of life as both comic and pathetic helped bring Beth Henley a Pulitzer Prize for this, her first full-length play. The McGrath sisters have their problems, and as Meg says toward the end of the play, "We've just got to learn how to get through these real bad days here."

In Act I Meg's old boy friend, Doc, pays a visit to Lenny.

> Doc: Here, some pecans for you.
> Lenny: Why, thank you, Doc. I love pecans.
> Doc: My wife and Scott picked them up around the yard.
> Lenny: Well, I can use them to make a pie. A pecan pie.

MISS'IPPI PECAN PIE

For a party of 8-10.
Preparation time: about 3 hours and 20 minutes, including cooling and chilling.

For the crust:
1/4 cup milk
1/2 teaspoon vinegar
1/4 cup vegetable shortening

1/4 cup margarine, softened
1 cup unbleached flour, plus extra flour for dusting

For the filling:
2 eggs or 4 ounces egg substitute
1 cup sugar
1/3 cup melted butter or margarine
1 cup light corn syrup
$1^1/2$ cup pecan (pronounced pi-`kän) halves
1/4 cup cognac

Preheat the oven to 450° F.

In a small bowl combine the milk and vinegar and set aside. In a separate small bowl, cream together the shortening and margarine until well blended. Place the flour in a large bowl. With a dough blender or 2 knives, cut the shortening mixture into the flour. Add the milk and mix well. The dough will be very sticky. Liberally dusting your hands and the dough with flour, work the dough until you can form a ball. On a floured surface, roll out the ball into a circle about 1/8" thick. Press the crust into a deep dish pie pan and trim the edges, leaving enough to form a decorative edge by pressing with your thumb and twisting the dough with your index finger, or by using the tynes of a fork. Line the crust with a circle of foil and fill with baking nuggets. Bake in the middle of the oven about 12 minutes. Remove from the oven; remove the nuggets and foil and allow the crust to cool, in the pan, to room temperature before filling.

Make the filling: In a large bowl, combine the eggs or egg substitute, sugar, butter or margarine and corn syrup. Beat well to blend. Add the pecans and cognac. Stir well.

Preheat the oven to 375° F.

When the crust has cooled to room temperature, stir the filling and pour it into the crust. Bake in the center of the oven until the crust is golden brown about 50 minutes. Cool in the pan on a wire rack. Refrigerate at least 2 hours to chill before cutting.

Serve Miss'ippi Pecan Pie chilled or at room temperature -- never hot, please!

Babe, who has shot her husband, needs a lawyer, and Barrette takes her case. In Act II he explains that they had met previously.

> Barrette: At the Christmas bazaar, year before
>   last. You were selling cakes and cookies
>   and . . . candy.
> Babe: Oh, yes! You bought the orange pound
>   cake.

BABE'S ORANGE POUND CAKE

For a party of 10-12.
Preparation time: about $1^1/2$ hours, including baking.

1 cup granulated sugar
1 cup confectioners sugar
1 cup butter or margarine, softened
4 eggs or 8 ounces egg substitute, beaten
3 cups unbleached flour
1/4 teaspoon (or less) salt
2 teaspoons baking powder
1 cup milk
1/2 teaspoon almond extract
Zest of 2 oranges, grated

Preheat the oven to 325° F.

In a medium bowl, combine the sugars. Place the butter or margarine in a large bowl and gradually add the sugar mixture, creaming until light and fluffy. Add the eggs or egg substitute and beat until smooth.

In a large bowl, sift the flour, baking powder and salt together twice. Add the flour mixture to the sugar mixture in 3 parts, alternating with the milk, beginning and ending with flour and beating on medium speed until blended after each addition. Add the almond extract and orange zest and blend by hand. Pour the batter into a greased and floured tube pan. Bake in the middle of the oven 1 hour and 10 minutes. Cool completely before removing from the pan.

Throughout the play, a proper celebration of Lenny's birthday is an issue. Finally, near the end of Act III, Meg asks for a ride to the bakery.

> Meg: Listen, Babe, I'll be right back with the cake. We're gonna have that celebration! Now, ah, if Lenny asks where I've gone, just say I'm . . . just say, I've gone out back to, ah, pick up some pawpaws! Okay?

If you want to help celebrate Lenny's birthday, a recipe for birthday cake is on page 27. But we know of no recipes for "pawpaws," which the dictionary spells "papaw," and defines as a yellowish, oblong, edible fruit with many seeds, from a tree of the custard-apple family.

CYRANO DE BERGERAC
By Edmund Rostand
(translated by Brian Hooker)
(1897)

A romantic extravaganza combining pathos and sentimentality, *Cyrano de Bergerac* features the magnificent gestures of a swashbuckling hero who has challenged some of the best actors of the twentieth century, including Jose Ferrer, whose performance with Eva Le Gallienne at the American Repertory Theatre in 1946 made a lasting impression. Who can forget Cyrano's fencing match with Viconte De Valvert, during which he composes a Ballade, defeating his opponent as he promises:

> Cyrano: Prince! Pray God, that is Lord of all,
> Pardon your soul, for your time has come!
> Beat-- pass-- fling you aslant, asprawl--
> Then, as I end the refrain -- Thrust home!

Act II takes place in the shop of Ragueneau, poet and pastry cook, where food is everywhere. Cooks appear with the most appealing of dishes: Fruits en gelée! Custard! Peacock rôte! Cakes and confections! Beef en casserole!

For your better appreciation of the scene, we invite you to try the following recipe.

BEEF BOURGIGNON DE BERGERAC

For a party of 6-8.
Preparation time: about 4 hours, including simmering.

This recipe may be prepared a day or two in advance (in fact, we think it's even better the second or third day) or prepared in stages, if time is a consideration.

1/2 pound salt pork or slab bacon
3 $^1/_4$ pound lean beef rump or chuck, cut into $1^1/_2$" chunks
1 tablespoon olive oil
2 cups dry red wine (a good French table wine)
2-3 cloves garlic, peeled and minced
1 tablespoon tomato paste
1/2 teaspoon thyme
1 bay leaf, crumbled
1 teaspoon dried basil
1-2 cups beef stock

For the garnish:
12 ounces fresh mushrooms, cleaned and stemmed
3 tablespoons butter or margarine
1 teaspoon olive oil
1 pound small white onions or a 16 ounce jar small whole onions
Sprigs of fresh parsley

For the sauce:
4 tablespoons unbleached flour
4 tablespoons butter or margarine, softened

Preheat the oven to 350° F.

Cut the pork or bacon into strips (*lardons*) about $1^1/4$" x $1/4$". In a medium saucepan bring 1 quart of water to boil, add the *lardons*, reduce heat and simmer, uncovered, 10 minutes. Drain the *lardons*, rinse with cold water and pat dry on paper towels.

Heat a large ($4^1/2$ quart size or larger) saucepan, add 1 tablespoon olive oil. When oil is hot, add the *lardons*, reduce heat slightly and cook over moderately high heat for about 12-15 minutes, turning the *lardons* to brown evenly. When the *lardons* are lightly browned and crisp, remove them from saucepan, drain on paper towels and set aside.

Pour off and reserve the pork fat remaining in the saucepan, leaving only a thin coating covering the bottom of the pan. When the fat begins to smoke over moderately high heat, add the first of several batches of beef. Don't crowd the beef in the pan. Cook the beef, turning frequently, to sear quickly on all sides. As each batch is seared, remove it from the pan with a slotted spoon and set aside. If necessary, add a bit of the reserved pork fat during the searing process.

When all the beef has been seared and removed from the pan, add the wine to the saucepan and scrape the bottom of the pan with a wooden spoon to mix any clinging bits of browned beef with the wine. Stir the garlic, tomato paste, thyme, bay leaf and basil into the liquid. Return the beef to the saucepan and add the *lardons*. If the wine is not sufficient to cover the beef, add enough beef stock to cover. Bring to a simmer.

Place the beef and liquid in a large oven-proof casserole (if your saucepan is not oven-proof), cover and place in lower 1/3 of oven. Simmer in oven $1^1/2$ to 2 hours, until the beef is tender when pierced with a sharp knife or fork. If the liquid begins to boil, reduce oven heat; the mixture should simmer but not boil. You may baste the beef occasionally, if you wish.

While the beef simmers in the oven, prepare the garnishes: If using fresh onions, blanch in boiling water for about 1 minute, drain, rinse in cold water and peel carefully. Make a small X at the stem end of each onion with a sharp knife; place the onions in a saucepan, cover with water and bring to a simmer. Cover and simmer about 20 minutes, until tender. Drain the onions and set aside. If using a jar of onions, do not cook; just drain the jar and set the onions aside.

Cut the mushrooms into 3/4" chunks. Heat a heavy skillet and melt together 2 tablespoons butter or margarine and 1 teaspoon olive oil. Add the mushrooms and sauté over moderately high heat about 3 minutes, shaking the skillet and moving the mushrooms around with a wooden spoon to brown evenly. Remove the mushrooms from the skillet and set aside.

Add the remaining 1 tablespoon butter or margarine to the juices remaining in the skillet. When the butter is melted, add the onions and sauté over moderately high heat about 3 minutes. Remove the onions from skillet and add to the mushrooms.

Assemble Beef Bourgignon de Bergerac: When the beef comes out of the oven, use a baster to remove as much of the liquid as possible from the casserole to a saucepan. If you have less than $3^1/2$ cups liquid, add enough beef stock to make that amount. Add the mushrooms and onions to the casserole and mix thoroughly with the beef.

Make the sauce: In a small mixing bowl blend 4 tablespoons flour with 4 tablespoons softened butter or margarine to make a smooth paste (roux). Bring the liquid in the saucepan to simmer. Add 5 or 6 tablespoons of the liquid to the roux and blend with a wire whisk until very smooth. Add the roux to the simmering liquid and return to simmer, stirring constantly. When the liquid is thick and bubbly, pour it over the beef and vegetables, stirring gently to coat evenly.

Cover the casserole and return it to the oven for about 10 minutes. Remove from the oven, garnish with the fresh parsley and serve immediately; or allow to cool, uncovered, for about 1 hour, cover and refrigerate.

Serve Beef Bourgignon de Bergerac with rice or mashed potatoes, a green salad, a full-bodied French red wine and -- to be faithful to the spirit of Cyrano -- French bread.

In Act II Ragueneau, the poet, gives his recipe for
Almond Tarts:

> Beat your egg, the yolks and white,
>   Very light.
> Mingle with their creamy fluff
>   Drops of lime-juice, cool and green;
> Then pour in almonds, just enough.
>
> Dainty patty-pans, embraced.
>   In puff-paste--
> Have these ready within reach;
>   With your thumb and finger, pinch
>   Half an inch.
> Up around the edge of each--
>
> Into these, a score or more,
>   Slowly pour
> All your store of custard; so
>   Take them, bake them golden-brown--
>   Now sit down!
> Almond tartlets, Ragueneau!

Making now some alteration
Plus more detailed explanation
(Due in part to Ed's frustration
   with poetic limitation,

or maybe Hooker's bold translation)
We offer you our own creation
For your hearty degustation.

ALMOND TARTLETS RAGUENEAU

For a party of 6.
Preparation time: about 2 ^{1}/2 hours, including baking and slight cooling.

For the crusts:
1/2 cup milk
1 teaspoon vinegar
2 cups unbleached flour plus extra flour for dusting
1 cup butter or margarine

For the custard:
4 eggs or 8 ounces egg substitute, lightly beaten
1 cup milk
Juice of 1 lime
1/2 cup sugar
2 tablespoons flour
1 teaspoon almond extract

Preheat the oven to 450° F.

In a small bowl, combine the milk and vinegar and set aside. In a large bowl, cut the butter into the flour with a dough blender or 2 knives and blend thoroughly. Add the milk and work together until completely blended. Dust your rolling surface, rolling pin and hands with flour. Divide the dough into 12 equal parts. Roll out each part into a 6" round. Press the rounds into the cups of a well greased (grease the top, too!) 12 cup (2 ^{1}/2") muffin tin. With your fingers, crinkle the dough which overhangs the top of each cup. Line each little crust with a circle of foil and fill with baking nuggets. Bake in the middle of the oven about 12 minutes. Remove the crusts from the oven, remove the nuggets and foil and allow the crusts to cool, in the tin, to room temperature before filling.

While the crusts bake, begin making the custard: Place the eggs or egg substitute in the top half of a double boiler, over, not in, cold water. Add 1/4 cup milk and stir to blend. In a small bowl or cup, combine the lime juice with the remaining milk and set aside. In another bowl, combine the sugar and flour and stir to mix thoroughly. Gradually add the sugar mixture to the egg mixture, stirring constantly until blended. Turn the heat to moderately high and add the remainder of the milk and the almond extract. Cook, stirring constantly, until the mixture begins to thicken in the bottom of the pan. Immediately reduce heat to medium and continue stirring until the mixture thickens to the consistency of custard (your spoon or whisk will leave a permanent trail when dragged across the top). Remove from heat and hot water and let cool, stirring occasionally.

Preheat the oven to 325° F.

When both the crusts and the custard are cooled, spoon the custard in equal portions into the crusts. Bake in the middle of the oven until crusts are golden brown, about 25-30 minutes. Cool a few minutes in the tin before serving warm.

THE DARK AT THE TOP
OF THE STAIRS
By William Inge
(1957)

Always writing about the obscure and lonely people of mid-America, Inge had his last success with *The Dark at the Top of the Stairs.* Only a few years earlier (with *Picnic,* 1953, *Come Back Little Sheba,* 1954, and *Bus Stop,* 1955) he had been a major contributor to America's developing drama. In this play, starring Theresa Wright and Pat Hingle as husband and wife Cora and Rubin Flood, Inge emphasizes the need for love and understanding amid heartbreaking discoveries of deception.

The scene is Oklahoma in the early 1920's. In Act I Cora tries to delay Rubin's sales trip by promising to get up early and cook bisquits. Later she uses the same promise to tempt Lottie and Morris to spend the night. In neither instance is Cora successful, but you can be with bisquits prepared from the recipes on pages 127 and 175.

Later in Act I Flirt Conroy, a flapper friend of the Flood's daughter, offers to cook the evening meal.

> Flirt: My mother makes me fix supper once a week, cook's night out. She says it's good for me to learn something about home-making. Isn't that crazy? The only thing I

know how to cook is salmon loaf. I learned how to make it in domestic science class. I've made salmon loaf every Monday night now for a whole year.

Laura in *The Glass Menagerie* may have taken the same domestic science class. (Inge and Tennessee Williams have been closely compared over the years.) You may check out her recipe on page 77.

In Act II we learn that Cora has served fried chicken for dinner with Lottie and Morris. Generously, she provides a bag for Lottie to take the leftovers her children won't eat: "They won't eat anything but the breast." We think that with our recipe they might be less picky.

CORA'S SKILLET-FRIED CHICKEN

For a party of 4-6.
Preparation time: about 1 hour.

1 frying chicken, cut up
1^1/2 cups unbleached flour
1/2 teaspoon (or less) salt)
Freshly ground black pepper, to taste
2 eggs or 4 ounces egg substitute, beaten
3/4 cup flat beer or water
Canola oil or safflour oil

For the gravy:
1 cup or more milk
Salt and freshly ground black pepper, to taste

Moisten the chicken pieces in cold water. Combine

the flour, salt and pepper and place in a plastic or paper bag large enough to hold the chicken. Add the chicken and shake the bag to coat on all sides with flour.

In a flat-bottomed bowl or pan, mix the eggs or egg substitute and beer or water. Remove the chicken pieces from the bag and gently dip them in the egg mixture to coat evenly. Return the chicken to the bag and turn gently until all the pieces are coated with flour. Remove the chicken from the bag and reserve the flour for gravy.

Heat a large skillet over medium heat and add enough oil to coat the bottom 1/2" to 1" deep. When the oil is very hot, carefully add the chicken in a single layer. Brown the chicken in batches, if necessary. Cook, turning once, until the batter is golden, about 5 minutes on each side. Lower heat to low, cover the skillet and cook until the crust is crisp and the chicken very tender when pierced with a fork, about 15-20 minutes. Remove the chicken from the skillet and drain on paper towels.

Make the cream gravy: Drain all but about 1 teaspoon of oil from the skillet. Add 1 tablespoon reserved flour and stir quickly to mix in bits of cooked batter remaining in the skillet. Add the milk and stir constantly until the desired thickness is reached, adding more milk as needed. Season to taste with salt and pepper.

Serve the chicken hot with mashed potatoes and cream gravy or cold, as Lottie eats it.

DEATH OF A SALESMAN
By Arthur Miller
(1949)

One of the best-known plays of twentieth-century America, *Death of a Salesman* illustrates Miller's tragedy of the common man. Willy Loman, his salesman, is recognized by audiences around the world for his "tentative" feelings about himself and his misguided striving for success and substance.

In Act II Willy's unsettled and troubled son Biff plans to see Bill Oliver, his old boss, to ask for backing for a business venture in sports. Afterwards, Willy will meet Biff and his other son, Happy, at Frank's Chop House to celebrate. Happy arrives first and talks to the waiter:

> Happy: You got a couple of nice lobsters?
> Stanley: Hundred per cent big.
> Happy: I want them with the claws.
> Stanley: Don't worry, I don't give you no mice.

Suddenly seeing his situation realistically, Biff abandons his plans and the Lomans do not get to eat their lobster dinner. Your celebrations, however, can be drastically different and end happily.

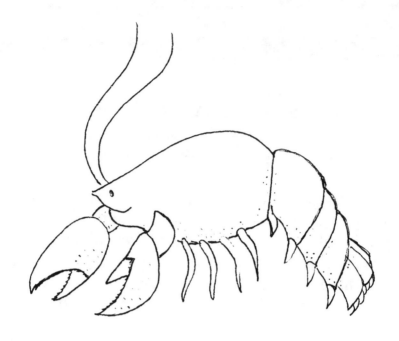

BOILED (STEAMED) LOBSTER

For a party of 4.
Preparation time: about 15 minutes.

4 whole, live Maine lobsters, about $1^1/4$ to $1^1/2$
    pounds each
1 cup unsalted butter (not margarine)

In a large pot with a tightly fitting lid, bring to a full
boil 2-3 inches of water. (The idea is to steam the
lobsters, rather than boil them in water.)

Carefully pick up one lobster at a time (do not
remove the rubber bands from the claws!), hold the
beast firmly behind the claws and drop it very
quickly, head first, into the pot. Cover, also very
quickly, and repeat the process with the next

lobster. (Unless your pot is very large indeed, you may want to use two pots, cooking two lobsters simultaneously in each.) Reduce heat to simmer and cook, tightly covered, about 11 minutes.

While the lobsters cook, clarify the butter: Cut the sticks into pieces and place in a small saucepan. Over low heat melt the butter completely. Remove from the heat and let stand a few minutes. The milk solids will settle to the bottom. Skim the clear butter fat from the top and strain through a double thickness of cheesecloth into a bowl. Discard the milk solids left in the pan and the sediment in the cheesecloth.

Remove the lobsters from the pot and drain. When the lobsters have cooled enough to be handled, serve with a small bowl of clarified butter for each guest (for dipping), corn on the cob and plenty of French or Italian bread. Your guests will thank you, too, if you provide each of them with a bib, a set of lobster tools (or a nutcracker and some kind of sharp pick) and a warm, damp washcloth. You might also want to have a stack of paper napkins handy.

Boiled Lobsters may also be served cold. After cooking, as above, plunge the lobsters into a pot of very cold water to arrest the cooking process. Refrigerate in the shells about 2 hours, then remove the meat from the shells and return it to the refrigerator until ready to serve or use in another recipe. If you are interested in lobster sandwiches, a recipe is on page 68.

THE DINING ROOM
By A. R. Gurney, Jr.
(1981)

Influenced by a wide variety of dramatists using many different theatrical forms, Gurney writes bitter-sweet comedies about white middle-class America. In *The Dining Room*, for example, six actors -- three men and three women -- play fifty-seven roles.

Although, as the title suggests, there is a lot of eating in the play, the dining room itself, its furnishings and the problems of his characters absorb Gurney's interest. Very little of the food served is identified -- a children's birthday party features ice cream; one meal inspires a grandfather to quip: "Finish your greens. They're good for your lower intestine," and at breakfast a mother requests poached eggs. We find poached eggs soothing and hope that Mother does, too.

POACHED EGGS

For a party of 6.
Preparation time: about 10 minutes.

6 eggs
1 teaspoon vinegar or 1/2 teaspoon lemon juice

Fill a large skillet almost to the top with water and bring to a full, rolling boil over high heat. Add the vinegar or lemon juice. Immediately reduce heat to simmer.

Meanwhile, gently break each egg into a cup or small bowl, being very careful not to break the yolk. When the water is still, hold the edge of each cup or bowl level with the surface of the water and gently tip in each egg. Leave as much space as possible between the eggs.

Allow the eggs to simmer until the whites appear to be firm, about 5 minutes. With a slotted spoon, carefully remove the eggs to a wet, smooth-surfaced colander (not a wire basket!) and drain about 2 minutes before serving. Discard any loose bits of egg white remaining in the skillet.

Serve the eggs on or with toast.

EAST LYNNE
By Clifton W. Tayleure
(1862)

For many Americans *East Lynne,* adapted from the novel by Mrs. Henry Wood, means sentimental melodrama. As one waggish critic wrote: "If all the scalding tears that fell/In sympathy for Isabel/Were gathered up throughout the years,/'Twould be an awful lot of tears." The plot is relatively simple for a melodrama. Convinced by Sir Francis Levison that her husband Archibald has been unfaithful, Isabel Carlyle runs off with the villain, who abandons her years later. Realizing the deception, Isabel returns in disguise to her former home, where Archibald has remarried, to serve as governess for her own child, who falls ill and dies in her arms. After dramatically revealing her own identity, Isabel also expires.

As a newlywed in Act I, Scene 3, Isabel is not accustomed to the wealth of Archibald's manor house. When asked by a servant what she should order for dinner, she responds: "Well, then, Miss Corney, you may tell them we'll have something to roast and something to boil."

The freedom allowed within the scope of this order may tempt the imagination as severely as the play tests our willing suspension of disbelief. We suggest roasting a readily available delicacy and boiling onions.

ROAST CHICKEN CARLYLE

For a party of 4.
Preparation time: about 1 hour, including baking.

3 tablespoons extra virgin olive oil
A 3 1/2-4 pound chicken, cut into serving pieces
3 medium sweet potatoes, peeled and cut into 1 1/2"
   cubes
2 cloves garlic, peeled and minced
1 teaspoon dried tarragon
1 teaspoon crushed oregano
Juice of 2 limes
Salt and freshly ground pepper, to taste

Preheat the oven to 400° F.

With 1 tablespoon of the oil, grease a large baking
dish.

In a large bowl, toss the chicken and potatoes with the remaining oil. Sprinkle with the garlic, tarragon, oregano, lime juice and salt and pepper and toss again. Place the chicken and potatoes in a single layer in the baking dish and loosely cover with foil. Bake in the middle of the oven 30 minutes. Remove the foil, turn the chicken over, replace the foil and bake 20 minutes more.

Before serving, brush with the pan juices. Serve with boiled onions.

BOILED ONIONS

For a party of 4.
Preparation time: about 25 minutes, including simmering.

4 medium white onions, peeled

Bring a large pot of water to a rolling boil. With a very sharp knife, cut away the root base at the bottom and any green appearing at the top of each onion. Plunge the onions into the boiling water, reduce heat to medium and cook until tender, about 20 minutes. Do not cook so long that the outer layers begin to fall away.

With a slotted spoon, remove the onions from the pot and drain before serving.

END OF SUMMER
By S. N. Behrman
(1936)

Few American dramatists have projected attitudes of detachment and expediency and maintained a sufficiently sophisticated wit to write successful comedies of manners. Behrman did just that, until the approach of World War II stirred his emotions. In *End of Summer* he chose a Victorian cottage in the area of Bar Harbor, Maine, as the scene for a confrontation between the very radical and the very rich who are ever the prey of the unscrupulous. Ina Claire and a young Van Hefflin had starring roles.

In Act II, Scene 2, as the genteel and wealthy woman contends with the verbal onslaught of a radical communist and an arrogant and opportunistic pyschiatrist, the butler intrudes to establish the true atmosphere of the domicile. He brings cocktails and sandwiches, to be followed by hors d'oeuvres.

Our suggestion for sandwich fixings would be lobsters trapped in neighboring Blue Hill Bay, southwest of Mount Desert (pronounced di-`sert) Island.

MAINE COAST LOBSTER SANDWICHES

For a party of 4.
Preparation time: about $1^1/2$ hours, including cooking, cooling and shelling the lobsters.

1 tablespoon melted butter or margarine
$1^1/2$ teaspoons fresh lime juice
3/4 pound Maine lobster meat, cooked and chopped
    into 1" chunks (from two $1^1/4$ pound Maine
    lobsters)
1/4 cup finely chopped celery
1/2 cup mayonnaise
1 teaspoon Dijon mustard
1 tablespoon minced fresh parsley or Italian parsley
1/2 teaspoon dried tarragon
Salt and freshly ground black pepper, to taste
4 large leaves green leaf or red leaf lettuce
4 Italian or other large sandwich rolls
2 tablespoons unsalted butter or margarine, for
    toasting the rolls
Fennel seed
Romano or Parmesan cheese, freshly grated

Cook the lobsters according to the recipe on page 60. When cool enough to handle, remove the meat from the shells and chop.

In a medium bowl, combine the melted butter or margarine and lime juice. Add the lobster and celery and toss well to coat evenly.

In a small bowl, combine the mayonnaise, mustard,

parsley, tarragon and salt and pepper. Mix well. Add the mayonnaise mixture to the lobster and toss. Spread the unmelted butter or margarine on the inside of each sandwich roll and toast, buttered side up, until golden.

Place about 1/2 cup of the lobster mixture on each lettuce leaf and place the leaves on the sandwich rolls. Sprinkle the sandwiches with the fennel seed and grated cheese and serve immediately with Chardonnay, not, please, as in the play, with cocktails.

THE FANTASTICKS
By Tom Jones and Harvey L. Schmidt
(1960)

Suggested by a play called *Les Romanesques* by Edmund Rostand, *The Fantasticks* is the longest running play in the history of New York's professional theatre. With its simple plot of innocent love, memorable music ("Try to Remember") and honestly naive style of presentation, *The Fantasticks* is a charming American success story. In the original cast Jerry Orbach starred as El Gallo, the narrator and master of the scene.

Halfway through the second act, Hucklebee and Bellomy, the two feuding fathers of the young lovers, recognize a common interest. They shake hands and sing:

>Plant a radish
>Get a radish.
>Never any doubt
>That's why I love vegetables;
>You know what you're about.

and conclude:

>Life is merry
>If it's very
>Vegetari-an
>A man who plants a garden
>Is a very happy man!

The song mentions turnips, carrots, brussels sprouts, kidney beans and cabbage. We didn't use them all, but we enjoy vegetables and the certainty of things that grow in the ground. We also believe that the following recipe can help make you a happy man -- or woman !

FANTASTICK BEAN ROLLS
WITH CILANTRO

For a party of 4.
Preparation time: about 1 hour, including baking.

1-2 cloves garlic, peeled and finely minced
3/4 cup chicken stock
1 medium onion (about 2" diameter), diced
1 teaspoon cumin seed, toasted and ground
1 teaspoon coriander seed, toasted and ground
$1^3/4$ cups (10 ounces) cooked, drained kidney beans
2 teaspoons chili powder
2 teaspoons tomato paste
1/4 cup chopped fresh cilantro
Salt and freshly ground black pepper, to taste
Six 6" corn tortillas
$1^1/2$ cups canned crushed tomatoes
2 ounces light cream cheese, cut into 1/2" pieces
1/2 cup sharp cheddar cheese, grated
3-4 scallions, sliced thinly on the diagonal
1/4 cup chopped pitted ripe olives
2-3 tablespoons low-fat sour cream or non-fat
    sour cream substitute

For the garnish:
Sprigs of fresh cilantro
1 orange, cut into wedges
Preheat the oven to 350° F.

In a skillet over medium heat, simmer the garlic in 2 tablespoons of the stock about 3 minutes. Add the onion and more stock as needed and cook, stirring occasionally, until the onion is translucent.

While the onion cooks, toast and grind the cumin and coriander seed. Add the cumin and coriander seed to the onion and stir. Stir in the beans and lower the heat. Mash the entire mixture with a sturdy fork to make a paste, adding stock as needed to prevent drying out (the onions need not be completely mashed). Add the chili powder and tomato paste and stir thoroughly. Stir in any remaining stock and half the cilantro. Season with the salt and pepper. Remove from heat.

Prepare the tortillas: Very lightly spray all the tortillas on both sides with non-stick spray. Arrange the tortillas in a stack and wrap tightly in foil which has also been lightly sprayed. Heat in the oven no more than 15 minutes.

In a saucepan heat the tomatoes and add the remaining cilantro. Simmer, stirring constantly, about 1 minute. Spray a baking dish (large enough to hold the rolled tortillas in a single layer) with non-stick spray. Spread a thin coating of tomatoes in the bottom of the baking dish.

Remove the tortillas from the oven. Spread 1/6 of the bean mixture (about 3 tablespoons) across the center of each tortilla. Dot the beans with pieces of cream cheese. Roll the tortillas into tubes about 1^1/$_2$" in diameter and arrange in the baking dish. Spread the remaining tomato mixture evenly over the tortillas, being sure the ends of each tube are well moistened. Top with the shredded cheese, scallions and olives. Dot with the sour cream.

Bake in the center of the oven until hot and bubbly, about 30 minutes.

Garnish with the fresh cilantro sprigs and orange wedges. Serve hot, with a crunchy garden salad (lettuce, carrots, red or green bell peppers, celery, radishes, etc.) and jalapeño cornbread.

FOR COLORED GIRLS
WHO HAVE CONSIDERED
SUICIDE/
WHEN THE RAINBOW IS ENUF
By Notzake Shange
(1976)

More poet than dramatist, and deeply involved in the political aspects of the Feminist Movement, Shange emphasizes the constant problems of Black American women and their enduring strength to face challenges. Called a "choreopoem" and based on some of Shange's early poems, *For Colored Girls* expresses the pain and anger of racial humiliation.

For Colored Girls tells the story of seven Black women. For the Lady in Brown the books of Toussaint L'Ouverture hold a special meaning. With him she dreamed of stowing away to New Orleans, where "we waz just gonna read & talk all the time/ & eat fried bananas."

The following recipe may or may not be exactly what the Lady in Brown had in mind, but we think you will enjoy bananas fried this way.

FRIED BANANAS

For a party of 6.
Preparation time: about 15 minutes.

6 bananas, slightly green
$1^1/2$ cups crushed cornflakes
3 tablespoons or more peanut oil
3 tablespoons light brown sugar
1 teaspoon ground cinnamon
1 tablespoon butter or margarine

Peel the bananas and split them in half, lengthwise. Spread the cornflakes closely on a sheet of waxed paper and firmly press the bananas, cut side down, into the cornflakes. Turn the bananas over and press a few cornflakes onto the uncut sides. Heat a large skillet over moderately high heat and add the oil. When the oil is hot, add the bananas, cut side down. Reduce heat to medium and cook until the bananas are golden brown on the cut side. Cook in batches, if necessary, adding more oil as needed. Turn the bananas over and immediately sprinkle the cut sides with the brown sugar and cinnamon and dot with the butter or margarine. Reduce heat to low, cover and cook until the butter or margarine has melted.

Serve immediately, cut side up, as a dessert with ice cream, or as a breakfast with sour cream, raspberry preserves and hotcakes (page 139), French toast (page 137), Breakfast Bisquits (page 127) or honey bisquits (page 175).

THE GLASS MENAGERIE
By Tennessee Williams
(1945)

This play launched Williams' career in the professional theatre and gave Laurette Taylor a triumphant final role as Amanda Wingfield. *The Glass Menagerie* did not win a Pulitzer Prize, but, with its touching story of loneliness and desperation, it still wins the hearts of a great many audiences.

In Scene 5, entitled "Anunciation," Tom Wingfield has finally invited a friend from the warehouse where he works to dinner -- tomorrow. Amanda, Tom's mother, worries about the immediacy of the event but soon becomes involved in planning.

> Amanda: What is the young man's name?
> Tom: His name is O'Connor.
> Amanda: That, of course, means fish--
> tomorrow is Friday! I'll have that salmon
> loaf -- with Durkee's dressing.

In Scene 6, O'Connor, by now elevated to the position of "the gentleman caller," arrives, and Amanda tries to promote Laura with the charm and persistence of the predatory mother.

> Tom: How about-- supper?
> Amanda: Honey, you go ask sister if supper is

ready! You know that sister is in full charge of supper!

Amanda, of course, is speaking for Jim O'Connor's benefit, and while her ploy fails, the salmon loaf is a dish well worthy of any gentleman caller.

INGENUE SALMON LOAF

For a party of 6.
Preparation time: about 1 hour, including baking.

1 1/2 cups coarse crumbs from fresh white bread
6 ounces light cream
3/4 pound uncooked salmon, finely chopped
1 tablespoon Dijon mustard
Salt and freshly ground black pepper, to taste
3 egg whites
Sprigs of fresh parsley, for garnish

Preheat the oven to 350° F.

In a medium saucepan combine the bread crumbs and cream. Cook over medium heat to form a hot paste. Add the salmon, mustard, and salt and pepper. Stir to blend. Remove the pan from the heat.

Beat the egg whites until stiff but not dry. Fold gently into the salmon mixture.

Transfer the mixture to a lightly buttered loaf pan (the pan should be about 3/4 full) and set the pan on several thicknesses of folded paper towels, in a larger pan of water (the water should reach at least 1/2 the way up the loaf pan).

Place both pans in the middle of the oven and bake until a knife inserted in center of loaf comes out clean, about 40 minutes.

Very carefully remove the pans from the oven and the loaf pan from the water pan. Let the loaf stand about 5 minutes in its pan before reversing onto a serving platter.

Garnish Ingenue Salmon Loaf with the fresh parsley and serve with steamed fresh broccoli and Parker House Rolls (page 20). Although a light, dry white wine would be good with this, Laura Wingfield might prefer iced tea Southern style-- with plenty of lemon and sugar.

THE GREEN PASTURES
By Marc Connelly
(1930)

Basing his play on the Negro folk tales collected by Roark Bradford, *Ol' Man Adam an' His Chillun*, Connelly dramatized a new interpretation of the Bible, complete with the Creation, the subsequent despair of De Lawd and His hopeful smile in the final scene. *The Green Pastures* has been criticized for not presenting an honest picture of Negro life. We like the food. The second scene shows a fish-fry in Heaven, in which God participates.

> Gabriel: Gangway! Gangway for de Lawd God Jehovah!

It is a happy affair, as God circulates among the Angels and Cherubs. One of the Cooks offers a fish sandwich, which God politely declines. We, however, offer you an opportunity to make your own decision relative to these heavenly treats.

DE LAWD'S REJECTS FISH SANDWICHES

For a party of 6.
Preparation time: about 20 minutes.

2 cups flaked cooked salmon (about 1 pound uncooked salmon fillet)
1/2 cup cracker crumbs (we prefer low sodium saltines)

2 eggs or 4 ounces egg substitute, beaten
1/8 teaspoon (or more) paprika
1/2 teaspoon grated fresh ginger root
Salt and freshly ground black pepper, to taste
2 tablespoons olive oil or canola oil
6 English muffins, split in half

For the garnish:
Ripe tomatoes, sliced
Ripe olives
Sprigs of fresh parsley

In a large bowl, combine the salmon, cracker crumbs, eggs, paprika, ginger root, and salt and pepper. Stir to mix well -- or mix it with your hands! Form the mixture into 6 balls of about 2" each and flatten into patties about 1/2" thick.

Heat a large non-stick skillet over medium heat and add enough oil to cover the bottom. When the oil is hot, add the fish patties in a single layer and cook until golden, about 4 minutes. Carefully turn over the patties with a spatula and cook about 4 minutes more.

While the patties cook, toast the muffins. Spread the muffins with honey mustard or homemade mayonnaise (page 181). Place a salmon pattie between the halves of each muffin. Garnish with the sliced ripe tomatoes, ripe olives and fresh parsley and serve with Eggs Mayonnaise (page 180).

Offered a glass of custard, God accepts without hesitation.

Gabriel: Little b'iled custard, Lawd?

But after His second sip a look of displeasure comes over His face. He can taste the eggs, the cream and sugar, but it needs more firmament.

Custard Maker: It's all we had, Lawd.   Dey ain't a drop in de jug.

God: Dat's all right. I'll jest r'ar back an' pass a miracle. [Choir stops singing.] Let it be some firmament . . . . I'm sick an' tired of runnin' out of it when we need it. Let it be a whole mess of firmament.

Well, the stage darkens; there is thunder and a downpour of rain. There is too much firmament, and the Cherubs are getting wet. Needing a place to drain the firmament, De Lawd creates mountains, valleys, oceans, lakes and rivers -- and finally, He says: "As a matter of fac' let dere be de earth." And the earth looks so nice: "Let dere be man." For your pleasure, we offer a recipe for the custard that caused it all.

FIRMAMENTED CUSTARD,
A DRINK FIT FOR DE LAWD

For a party of 6-8.
Preparation time: about $2^1/2$ hours, including chilling.

5 cups milk
3/4 cup sugar
1/4 teaspoon (or less) salt
8-10 egg yolks or 8 ounces egg substitute
1/2 cup firmament (dry sherry)*

Place the milk in the top of a double boiler over, not in, boiling water and heat until scalded (when tiny bubbles around the edge of the pan begin to pop). Do not allow the milk to boil!

Combine the sugar and salt and beat into the egg yolks or egg substitute. In a slow stream, pour the egg mixture into the milk, stirring constantly. Continue stirring until the mixture is about the texture of eggnog or buttermilk. Remove from heat and beat with a wire whisk to release steam and hasten cooling. Stir in the firmament. Refrigerate at least 2 hours to chill before serving in cups or small glasses.

*Now is your chance to play God -- add as much firmament as you wish!

[   ]

HARVEY
By Mary Ellen Chase
(1944)

Here is a whimsical comedy about a contented dipsomaniac, Elwood P. Dowd, and his friend Harvey, a pooka. In Act II, Scene 2, Elwood explains how they met:

> [One evening] as I started to walk down the street . . . I heard a voice saying, "Good evening, Mr. Dowd." I turned and there was this great white rabbit leaning against a lamp post. . . . Naturally, I went over to chat with him. . . . Finally, I said--"You have the advantage of me. You know my name and I don't know yours." Right back at me he said, "What name do you like?" . . . So I said, "Harvey," and this is the interesting part of the whole thing. He said, "What a coincidence! My name happens to be Harvey."

Harvey won a Pulitzer Prize and ran for four years with Frank Fay as Elwood P. Dowd and Josephine Hull as his dithering sister. In 1970 the Phoenix Theater staged a popular revival with James Stewart and Helen Hayes.

This quick and nutritious dish, loaded with fresh garden vegetables, would surely appeal to Harvey, but only Elwood P. Dowd could find a rabbit among the ingredients.

POOKA POT "RABBIT"

For a party of 4.
Preparation time: about 45 minutes.

4 tablespoons peanut oil
1 medium onion, coarsely chopped
1-2 cloves garlic, peeled and minced
1 green bell pepper, with membranes and seeds removed, coarsely chopped
2 medium carrots, scraped and sliced diagonally into 1/4" slices
1/2 teaspoon dried basil
1 teaspoon flour
1 rib celery, sliced diagonally into 1/4" slices
1 cup chicken stock
1 tablespoon tomato paste
1 tablespoon butter or margarine
8 ounces extra firm tofu, cut into 1" cubes
4-5 large mushrooms, with stems trimmed, cut into 1/2" chunks
2-3 scallions, sliced diagonally into 1/4" slices (white and green parts)
1/2 teaspoon dried red pepper flakes
Salt and freshly ground black pepper, to taste
1/4 cup chopped fresh parsley
Sprigs of fresh parsley, for garnish

Heat a large skillet over medium heat and add 2 tablespoons of the oil. When the oil is hot, add the onion and sauté until golden, about 5 minutes. Add the garlic and sauté 1 minute. Add the bell pepper, carrots and basil and sauté about 3 minutes. Sprinkle the flour evenly over the vegetables and toss to coat. Add the celery, stock, tomato paste and salt and pepper. Reduce heat to simmer, cover and cook about 10 minutes.

In a separate large skillet, heat the remaining oil and in it melt the butter or margarine. Add the tofu and mushrooms and sauté over medium heat, tossing to brown evenly, about 3 minutes. Add the scallions and red pepper flakes. Sauté until the tofu and mushrooms are evenly golden, about 3 minutes. Using a slotted spoon, transfer the tofu, mushrooms and scallions from the oil to the vegetable mixture. Stir in the chopped parsley and cook, uncovered, over medium heat until the carrots, peppers and celery are tender-crisp. Garnish with the fresh parsley and serve over rice or pasta.

I REMEMBER MAMA
By John Van Druten
(1944)

Marlon Brando made his Broadway debut in this popular adaptation of Kathryn Forbes' novel, *Mama's Bank Account.* The audience finally learns that Marta ("Mama") has never had a bank account, but the idea of one gives a sense of security to the Norwegian family living in San Francisco in 1910.

When Katrin, a daughter, becomes disheartened because her stories are always being rejected by magazine editors, Mama decides to seek the advice of a celebrated woman writer who is visiting San Francisco. She accosts her in her hotel and, with the promise of a recipe for Kjödboller -- meatballs with sauce -- maneuvers her into reading Katrin's stories.

> Mama:　When you make the meat-balls you drop them in boiling stock. Not water. That is one of the secrets.
> F. D. Moorhead:　Ah!
> Mama:　And the cream sauce. That is another secret. It is half <u>sour</u> cream, added at the last.

As usual, Mama gets what she wants, and we are convinced that you, too, will enjoy her recipe.

MARTA'S *KJÖDBOLLER* (MEATBALLS)

For a party of 8 (about 48 meatballs).
Preparation time: about 1 hour, including simmering.

3 slices dry toasted bread
8 cups beef or chicken stock
2 tablespoons butter or margarine
2 shallots, peeled and finely minced
2 pounds extra lean ground beef
1/4 pound extra lean ground pork
2 egg whites
3 tablespoons minced parsley
Salt and freshly ground black pepper, to taste
1/8 teaspoon allspice
1/4 teaspoon freshly ground nutmeg
1/8 teaspoon ground cloves

For the sauce:
4 tablespoons butter or margarine
3 tablespoons unbleached flour
1 cup or more milk
1 cup sour cream
2 shallots, peeled and finely minced
1 bay leaf
Salt and cayenne pepper, to taste

In a flat-bottomed bowl or pan, cover the toast with 1/2 cup stock and let stand until moistened.

Heat a small skillet over moderately high heat and add the butter or margarine. When melted and bubbly, add the shallots and sauté, stirring frequently, until golden.

In a large bowl, combine the beef and pork (to be faithful to Marta's "secret recipe," you should grind the beef and pork together 6 times), the shallots, egg whites, parsley, salt, pepper, allspice, nutmeg and cloves. Add the moistened toast, breaking it up and mixing well. With moistened hands, shape the mixture into 1" balls.

In a large pot, bring the remaining 7 $1/2$ cups stock to a boil. Drop the meatballs into the stock, in batches if necessary, cover, reduce heat to simmer and cook 20 minutes.

While the meatballs simmer, prepare the sauce: In a skillet over medium-low heat, blend the butter or margarine and flour to make a smooth paste (roux). Add the shallots, milk, cream and bay leaf. Season with the salt and cayenne pepper. Cook, stirring constantly, until the shallots are tender and the sauce has thickened. (If the sauce becomes too thick before the shallots are tender, add more milk as needed.) Remove the bay leaf.

Remove Marta's Meatballs from the stock, cover with the cream sauce and serve hot.

IDIOT'S DELIGHT
By Robert E. Sherwood
(1936)

A veteran of World War I, Sherwood promoted pacifism in his plays until Hitler aroused the anger and righteous determination that burst forth in *There Shall Be No Night* (1940). *Idiot's Delight* was vividly anti-war, but both plays were anti-Fascist, and both plays served as vehicles for Alfred Lunt and Lynn Fontanne.

The scene is the Hotel Monte Gabriele in the Italian Alps, where the gathered people await the coming war--Harry Van and the chorus girls; Mr. and Mrs. Cherry, the English honeymooners; Dr. Waldersee, the German scientist; Achille Weber, the munitions maker and his companion, Irene. These varied characters allow Sherwood great opportunity to speak his mind.

As disaster approaches in Act II, the English honeymooners are beginning to feel the pressure.

> Mrs. Cherry: We didn't really dine at all. We merely looked at the minestrone and the Parmesan cheese -- and we felt too depressed to eat anything.

MINESTRONE WITH PARMESAN CHEESE

For a party of 8.
Preparation time: about $3^1/2$ hours, including simmering.

1 cup dry navy beans
3 tablespoons extra virgin olive oil
1 leek, washed, cleaned and chopped (white part only)
1-2 large cloves garlic, peeled and minced
1 cup scraped, chopped carrots
2 cups chopped cabbage
1 can (28 ounces) crushed tomatoes in tomato purée
1 cup beef stock
1 teaspoon dried basil
1 cup frozen peas
1/2 pound elbow macaroni, cooked *al dente*
1/4 cup chopped fresh Italian parsley
Parmesan cheese, freshly grated, for topping

Cover the beans with cold water and soak overnight. Drain the beans, rinse in cold water and place in a large saucepan. Add 6 cups cold water and bring to a boil over high heat. Immediately reduce heat to simmer and cook until the beans are just tender. Remove from heat, drain, cover and refrigerate the beans.

Heat a large pot over moderately high heat and add the oil. When hot, add the leek, garlic, carrots, cabbage and tomatoes and their purée and cook, stirring occasionally, about 3 minutes. Add the beef stock and basil. Reduce heat to simmer, cover and cook about $2^1/2$ hours (do not boil!). Add the peas. Place the beans in a small saucepan and add about 1/2 cup liquid from the cooking pot. Bring the beans to a boil and add to the cooking pot. Add the macaroni and parsley and season with salt and pepper. Simmer to heat through.

Pour the soup into a heated tureen. (Also heat the individual bowls by allowing hot water to stand in them 10 minutes before serving.) Sprinkle the soup with Parmesan cheese. Serve with garlic bread or crusty Italian bread.

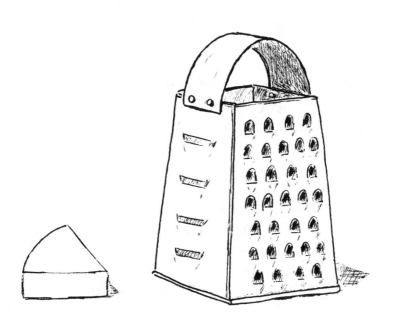

𝕬𝕬𝕬𝕬𝕬𝕬𝕬𝕬𝕬𝕬𝕬𝕬𝕬𝕬𝕬𝕬𝕬𝕬𝕬𝕬𝕬𝕬

THE IMPORTANCE
OF BEING EARNEST
By Oscar Wilde
(1895)

Wilde's masterpiece of drawing-room melodrama is a favorite with actors and audiences. One memorable revival took place in New York in 1947, with John Gielgud both staging the play and acting the role of John Worthing.

Who can forget the brilliant repartee and charming affectations that occur in Algernon's flat in Half-Moon Street! And who can forget the cucumber sandwiches, ordered especially for Lady Bracknell and Gwendolen, who is "devoted to bread and butter," and yet consumed by Jack and Algernon before these guests arrive.

> Algernon (picking up empty plate): Good heavens! Lane! Why are there no cucumber sandwiches: I ordered them specially.
> Lane (gravely): There were no cucumbers in the market this morning, sir. I went down twice.
> Algernon: No cucumbers!
> Lane: No, sir. Not even for ready money.

We found some cucumbers for ready money, however, and invite you to enjoy them with your afternoon tea.

ALGERNON'S CUCUMBER SANDWICHES

For a party of 6.
Preparation time: about 10 minutes.

1 large cucumber, peeled and sliced paper thin
12 slices fresh white, whole wheat or rye bread
Butter or margarine
Mayonnaise (optional)
Dijon mustard (optional)

For the garnish:
6 large leaves green or red leaf lettuce
Sprigs of fresh watercress or parsley

Cut the crusts from the bread slices and spread one side of each slice very lightly with butter or margarine and/or mayonnaise or mustard. Divide the cucumber slices into 6 equal portions and arrange a portion evenly on the spread side of 6 bread slices. Top with the remaining bread slices. Cut each sandwich twice diagonally, to form 4 equal triangles. Secure with toothpicks, if necessary. Arrange the sandwiches on the lettuce leaves and garnish with the watercress or parsley. Serve immediately.

THE KING AND I
By Richard Rodgers
and Oscar Hammerstein, II
(1951)

The authors based this much-loved work on a novel by Margaret Landon entitled *Anna and the King of Siam*. With Gertrude Lawrence as Anna Leonowens, the governess engaged to tutor Siam's crown prince, and Yul Brynner as the recalcitrant King Rama II, this musical played for 1,246 performances in New York. Jerome Robbins' choreography, particularly the stylized ballet of "The Small House of Uncle Thomas," is also memorable.

Concerned with individual freedom and modern democratic ways, Anna befriends the young concubine Tuptim, who is distraught over her fate. When, in Act II, Scene 4, the King discovers that Tuptim has run away, he asks Anna her opinion.

> Anna: Your Majesty, of what interest to you is one girl like Tuptim? She is just another woman, as a bowl of rice is just another bowl of rice, no different from any other bowl of rice.

Anna, of course, does not believe her own argument, but her image is apt for Siam (Thailand since 1939), which is the fifth largest producer of rice in the world.

And Anna's analogy is not quite accurate either; we have found that one bowl of rice can be as different from the next as one girl from another. (For a distinctly different rice dish, try the Caribbean Rice on page 178.) Americans have been conditioned by manufacturers and advertisers to demand grains of rice that separate from each other on the plate. In Asia rice must hold together in clumps which do not fall apart when lifted with chopsticks or fingers! Rice cooked according to the following recipe will be suitable for the fork, which the Thais use, or whatever utensil you prefer.

ANNA'S RICE

For a party of 6.
Preparation time: 25-30 minutes, including simmering.

2 cups uncooked white rice
4 cups cold water

Place the rice in a large saucepan and add the water. Bring to a full boil over high heat. Immediately reduce heat to simmer and cover tightly. Cook 15 minutes. Remove from heat and let stand, still covered, 5-10 minutes, until the rice has absorbed any liquid remaining in the pan.

Western cultures frequently serve rice as a side dish. We suggest that you serve your rice with a classic pork dish of Thailand.

KING RAMA'S PORK

For a party of 6.
Preparation time: 15 minutes or less.

3 tablespoons peanut oil
3-4 large garlic cloves, peeled and finely minced
$1^1/2$ pounds boneless pork loin or butt, very thinly
    sliced into $1^1/2$" strips with excess fat removed
1/2 cup diagonally sliced (1/4") scallions (white and
    green parts)
3 tablespoons oriental fish sauce (available in
    oriental markets)
1/4 cup chopped fresh cilantro
Salt and freshly ground black pepper, to taste

For the garnish:
$1^1/2$ cups shredded lettuce
1 ripe tomato, cut into 6 wedges
1 orange, cut into 6 wedges
1 small cucumber, thinly sliced

Heat a wok or a large skillet over moderately high
heat and add the oil. When the oil is hot, add the
garlic and sauté about 30 seconds. Add the pork
and sauté, tossing constantly with a wooden spoon
or wok paddle, about 4 minutes. Add the scallions
and continue tossing about 1 minute. Add the fish
sauce, cilantro and salt and pepper and toss to heat
through, about 1 minute. Garnish with the lettuce,
tomato, orange wedges and cucumber. Serve King
Rama's Pork hot with Anna's Rice and hot tea.

LIFE WITH FATHER
By Howard Lindsay and Russel Crouse
(1939)

This extremely popular comedy adapted from Clarence Day's stories about his family ran for 3,224 performances, breaking all records of the time. With the slightest of plot lines -- the only continuing action is the attempt to get Father baptized -- the play was described by one reviewer as "a series of tableaux rather than an orthodox dramatic work." But people flocked to see it.

Concerned with the daily affairs of an upper-class New York family, scenes at the dining room table are not uncommon. In Act I, Scene 1, Vinnie, the mother, explains how breakfast should be served, and the audience watches the serving of fruit, oatmeal, milk, bacon and eggs and coffee. The same activity is repeated in Act II, Scene 2. In Act III, Scene 2, Father is surprised at breakfast with bisquits and kippers.

The most elegant part of the Day family's cuisine, however, is not served during the play but only mentioned in passing. In Act II, Scene 2, Vinnie says that she "promised Mrs. Whitehead to send over [their cook's] recipe for floating island pudding."

This is, indeed, a delightful dessert.

FLOATING ISLAND PUDDING

For a party of 6-8.
Preparation time: about 30 minutes, plus 2-3 hours if chilling.

4 egg whites
1¼ cups sugar
5 cups milk
1/4 teaspoon (or less) salt
8-10 egg yolks or 8-10 ounces egg substitute
1/2 cup dry sherry

In a large bowl, beat the egg whites until stiff but not dry. Gradually beat in 1/3 cup of the sugar. Pour the milk into a large skillet and heat until scalded (when tiny bubbles around the edge of the pan begin to pop). Do not allow the milk to boil! Using a tablespoon, gently drop the egg whites in dollops into the milk. Poach about 2 minutes, turn the whites over and poach about 2 minutes more. Gently remove the cooked egg whites (meringues) from the milk and drain on paper towels.

Pour the milk into the top of a double boiler over, not in, boiling water and heat until scalded. Again, do not allow the milk to boil!

Combine the remaining sugar and salt and beat into the egg yolks or egg substitute. In a slow stream, pour the egg mixture into the milk, stirring constantly. Continue stirring until the mixture is about the texture of eggnog or buttermilk. Remove from heat and beat with a wire whisk to release steam and hasten cooling. Stir in the sherry.

Spoon the custard into individual serving dishes and allow to cool. Top each dish with a meringue (the cooked egg whites) and chill at least 2 hours before serving.

For an alternative style of serving, spoon the custard into an oven-proof serving dish and allow to cool. Preheat the oven to 350° F. Arrange the meringues evenly on top of the custard. Place the dish in a pan of ice water and place both pans in the oven. Cook just until the tips of the meringues begin to brown, about 10-12 minutes. Serve immediately. We like this pudding with Babe's Orange Pound Cake (page 46).

LILIOM
By Ferenc Molnar
(1921)

American audiences know this Hungarian play better through its adaptation as a musical-- Rodgers and Hammerstein's *Carousel* (1945). Liliom is a carnival barker, arrogant and popular with the girls. When Julie falls in love with him and needs money for the birth of their child, Lilion falls in with bad company, is almost caught in a robbery and kills himself.

When his daughter Louise is sixteen, Liliom is allowed a brief return to earth. In Scene 7, as Julie and Louise are having soup, Liliom appears. Neither Julie nor, of course, Louise recognizes him.

Julie: Sit down and rest. My daughter is bringing you some soup.

They eat together.

HUNGARIAN TOMATO SOUP

For a party of 8.
Preparation time: about 2 hours and 45 minutes, including simmering.

1 pound beef stew meat, excess fat removed
5 ripe tomatoes, peeled, seeded and minced
1 rib celery, minced

1 leek, washed and minced (white part only)
2 carrots, scraped and minced
1 tablespoon paprika
Salt and freshly ground black pepper, to taste

Place the stew meat in a large pot and add 6 cups cold water. Bring to a boil over high heat. Immediately reduce heat to simmer, cover and cook until tender, about 2 hours. Remove the meat, reserving the liquid in the stew pot. Cut the meat into small pieces and return to the stew pot.

Place the tomatoes, celery, leek and carrots in another large pot and add enough of the liquid from the stew pot just to cover the vegetables. Bring to a boil over high heat. Immediately reduce heat to simmer and cook until tender, about 20-25 minutes. Place the vegetables and their liquid in a blender and puré, or force through a sieve. Add the purée to the stew pot and bring to a simmer. Cook over low heat, stirring occasionally and skimming off any foam that forms on the surface, about 10 minutes. Add the paprika and salt and pepper and serve hot with French bread, toast or fried bread.

$❦$❦$❦$❦$❦$❦$❦$❦$❦

THE LITTLE FOXES
By Lillian Hellman
(1939)

Tallulah Bankhead played the role of Regina in the original production of this exposé of selfishness, greed and cruelty in a Southern family during the spring of 1900. With a superior grasp of melo-dramatic technique and a determination to draw morals in her plays, Hellman foreshadowed the strength that she would display both in the theatre and as a writer condemned by the House Committee on UnAmerican Activities.

As the play opens, the Hubbards -- Regina Giddens and her brothers Oscar and Leo -- are extremely happy with the deal they have just made with a Northern businessman. Exuberantly, Cal tells Addie, the cook, that Regina's daughter, Zan, "had two helpings frozen fruit cream and she tell that honored guest that you make the best frozen fruit cream in all the South." In the Southern tradition, this is a _very_ rich concoction. Serve it sparingly!

ADDIE'S FROZEN FRUIT CREAM

For a party of 8 or more.
Preparation time: about 4 hours and 20 minutes, including freezing and chilling.

3/4 cup dried apricots
1/2 cup sugar

1 teaspoon gelatin
2 cups whipping cream
2-3 drops almond extract
1/4 cup chopped peanuts
2 tablespoons chocolate shavings

Chill a shallow freezer-safe pan in the freezer.

Place the apricots and 1/4 cup of the sugar in a small saucepan. Add enough water to cover the apricots and bring to a boil over high heat. Cook, stirring frequently, about 10 minutes. Drain the apricots and reserve the cooking liquid. Chill 2 tablespoons of the liquid.

Purée the apricots in a blender. Soak the gelatin in the chilled liquid about 5 minutes. Reheat 2 more tablespoons of the cooking liquid and add the gelatin mixture, stirring to dissolve. Stir the gelatin into the apricots and chill until almost set, about 20 minutes.

Beat 1 cup of the whipping cream until soft peaks just begin to form. Beat in, a bit at a time, 3 tablespoons of the remaining sugar and continue beating until the cream is fluffy and firm peaks form. Gently fold the whipped cream into the apricots. Spread the mixture evenly in the chilled pan. Cover the pan tightly with foil and place in the freezer on top of other frozen packages, not on a shelf. Freeze at least 2 hours.

About 1^1/2 hours before serving, remove the pan from the freezer, and let stand at room temperature about 30 minutes. Transfer the apricot cream from the pan to a large bowl. In a separate bowl, beat the remaining 1 cup whipping cream until soft peaks just begin to form. Add the remaining 1 tablespoon of sugar and the almond extract and continue beating until the cream is fluffy and firm peaks form. Gently fold the whipped cream into the apricot cream. Refrigerate about 1 hour before serving.

Spoon the Frozen Fruit Cream into chilled bowls, sprinkle with chopped peanuts and/or chocolate shavings and serve with cookies, cake and/or fresh fruit. (Frozen Fruit Cream also makes a luscious topping for chilled cream pies and an impressive frosting for nut cakes, carrot cakes and spice cakes.)

* * *

Later in the play, Zan has been sent to Baltimore to bring her ailing father, Horace, home from the hospital in order that he may be persuaded to support the schemes of Regina and her brothers. As Act III opens, Horace and Oscar's naively sweet wife, Birdie, begin to explain things to Zan. Addie enters with a carafe of elderberry wine and a plate of cookies.

> Zan: Addie! A party! What for?
> Addie: Nothing for, I had the fresh butter, so I made the cakes, and a little elderberry does the stomach good in the rain.

And, eaten in moderation, the little cake-cookies won't do you any harm, either.

FOXY LITTLE CAKE-COOKIES

For a party of 8 (about 16 cake-cookies).
Preparation time: about 50 minutes, including baking.

1/3 cup packed light brown sugar
1^1/3 cups granulated sugar
1/2 cup butter or margarine
1/4 cup canola oil or safflour oil
2 eggs or 4 ounces egg substitute, slightly beaten
3/4 cup quick oats
2 ^{1}/2 cups unbleached flour
1 teaspoon baking soda
1/8 teaspoon (or less) salt
3/4 cup creamy peanut butter
1 teaspoon vanilla

Preheat the oven to 375° F.

Mix the sugars and cream the mixture with the butter or margarine. Mix in the oil. Add the eggs and blend well.

In another bowl combine the oats, flour, baking soda and salt. Stir the oat mixture into the sugar mixture. Add the peanut butter and vanilla and mix well. The batter will be very stiff. Using about 2 tablespoons per cake-cookie, spoon the batter onto a greased cookie sheet (about 8 cookies to each sheet) and bake in the middle of the oven until golden, about 15 minutes. Remove from the oven and let stand on the sheet 2-3 minutes. Using a spatula, move the cookies to a wire rack and cool completely before serving with milk or coffee.

A LITTLE NIGHT MUSIC
By Hugh Wheeler and Stephen Sondheim
(1973)

With such musicals as *Company* (1970), *Sweeney Todd* (1979), and *Sunday in the Park With George* (1984), composer-lyricist Sondheim experiments with both form and subject matter. In *A Little Night Music* he follows the efforts of a middle-aged lawyer to recapture his youth through a young bride while being haunted by a past lover, Desiree.

In Act II, Scene 1, Desiree's mother makes a profound observation while passing on some unimpeachable advice:

> Mrs. Arnfeldt: To lose a lover or even a husband or two during the course of one's life can be vexing. But to lose one's teeth is a catastrophe. Bear that in mind, child, as you chomp so recklessly into that ginger snap.

In Scene 4 of this act, these sophisticated people presumably enjoy an excellent meal, but the writer, either from a concern for the tightness of his dialogue or a disdain for our culinary interests, fails to give audiences even a hint of the delicacies consumed. We do know, however, that they eat ginger snaps, and with this recipe you can chomp as recklessly as you wish.

RECKLESS GINGER SNAPS

About 3 dozen cookies.
Preparation time: about 30 minutes, including baking.

3/4 cups butter or stick margarine
2 cups sugar
2 egg whites
1/2 cup molasses
2 teaspoons vinegar
3 3/4 cups unbleached flour
1 1/2 teaspoons baking soda
3 teaspoons ground ginger
1 teaspoon ground cinnamon
1/4 teaspoon ground nutmeg

Preheat the oven to 350° F.

In a large bowl, cream the butter or margarine and the sugar. Stir in the egg whites, molasses and vinegar. Into another large bowl, sift together the flour, baking soda, ginger, cinnamon, cloves and nutmeg. Add the flour mixture to the butter mixture and mix until well blended. Using your hands, form the dough into balls about 1 1/2" in diameter. Arrange the balls 2 inches apart on greased cookie sheets and bake in the middle of the oven about 15 minutes. Cool 4-5 minutes on the cookie sheets, then transfer to waxed paper.

Serve the ginger snaps warm or at room temperature.

THE MADWOMAN OF CHAILLOT
By Jean Giraudoux
(1943)

Perhaps the best known French playwright between the world wars, Giraudoux delighted in dramatizing familiar events and exploring their obvious contradictions. *The Madwoman of Chaillot* was written shortly before his death in 1944 and first produced in New York in 1948. Like his other plays, it reveals his profound commitment to humanitarian ideals.

Act II is set in the cellar of the Countess' house, where she holds court, pours tea and serves cake and honey.

MADWOMAN TEA CAKES

For a party! (about 30 tea cakes).
Preparation time: about 1 hour, including baking.

1 cup sifted cake flour
3/4 cup sifted unbleached flour
2 teaspoons baking powder
1 cup sugar
1/2 cup butter or margarine
1/4 cup light cream cheese
1/4 cup milk
2 tablespoons whipping cream

2 tablespoons lemon juice
Zest of 1 lemon, grated
3 egg whites
Confectioners sugar, for topping
Honey or purée of fresh strawberries, for garnish

Preheat the oven to 350° F.

Into a medium bowl, resift the cake flour and unbleached flour together with the baking powder. Resift again. Into a small bowl, sift the sugar. In a large bowl, cream the butter or margarine and the cream cheese until soft. Gradually, add the sugar and blend until very light. Mix together the milk and whipping cream. Add the flour mixture to the sugar mixture in three parts, alternating with the milk mixture, beginning and ending with the flour and beating until smooth after each addition. Add the lemon juice and zest. Stir to blend thoroughly.

In a medium bowl, beat the egg whites until stiff but not dry. Lightly fold into the batter.

Insert paper baking cups into 2 1/2" muffin tins and fill each cup 1/2 full of batter. (If all cups are not filled, fill empty cups 1/2 full of warm water.) Bake in the middle of the oven until a toothpick inserted in the center of a cake comes out clean, about 30 minutes.

Remove the cakes from the tins and cool in the paper cups until ready to serve. Sprinkle with the confectioners sugar. Serve with the honey or strawberry purée and hot tea (we like chamomile--no caffeine!).

THE MALE ANIMAL
By James Thurber and Elliot Nugent
(1940)

The celebrated essayist and cartoonist collaborated with his Phi Psi fraternity brother, a playwright and actor, in this serio-comic study of freedom of expression on a college campus. College life may have changed since 1940, but the problems of the young idealist pressured to surrender to "prejudice and dictation" have not.

The scene is Professor Tommy Turner's living room, where everyone is preparing to attend a rally prior to the big Michigan-Midwestern University football game. (The authors attended Ohio State University.) Tommy's wife, Ellen, is trying to get her guests organized: "Shall we go into the dining room? It's only a salad. We're going to eat afterwards."

All we know about Ellen's salad is that the wife of the university trustee says: "Eat your vegetables, Ed." It would be difficult to find more vegetables together in one place than in our Salad 13 Plus, and you can make a good impression on your guests by including, as Ellen does, sherbet and coffee on your menu.

SALAD 13 PLUS

For a party of 6.
Preparation time: about 30 minutes.

1/2 cup raw broccoli florettes, separated into bite-
    sized pieces
1/2 cup raw cauliflour florettes, in bite-sized pieces
1 sweet red bell pepper, coarsely chopped
1 rib celery, cut on the diagonal into 1/4" slices
1 small summer squash, coarsely chopped or sliced
    into 1/8" rounds
2 carrots, sliced into 1/8" rounds
3-4 radishes, thinly sliced
2-3 tablespoons raisins
2 cups small cooked shrimp
1 tablespoon slivered almonds
1 cup drained mandarin orange sections
2-3 tablespoons salad dressing of choice
2-3 hard boiled eggs, thinly sliced (optional)
1 whole ripe avocado
6 leaves green leaf or red leaf lettuce

In a large serving bowl, toss together the broccoli,
cauliflour, bell pepper, celery, squash, carrots,
radishes and raisins. Add the shrimp, almonds,
orange sections and about 2/3 of the dressing and
gently toss again.

Place a lettuce leaf on each plate and top with
salad. Peel, pit and thinly slice the avocado. On top
of the salad, arrange the egg and avocado slices
and drizzle on the remaining dressing. Serve
immediately with fresh bread. (Pumpernickel is
delicious with this salad!)

MAN AND SUPERMAN
By George Bernard Shaw
(1903)

As critic and reformer, Shaw spoke his mind in plays for more than fifty years. Using the ideas of Schopenhauer, Bergson and Nietzsche in *Man and Superman: A Comedy and a Philosophy* to create a superman, he accomplished his task with a Shavian twist.

It is evening in the Sierra Nevadas when Shaw's protagonist, John Tanner, meets the Brigand chief.

> Mendoza: I am a brigand; I live by robbing the rich.
> Tanner: I am a gentleman; I live by robbing the poor.   Shake hands.
> [A few moments pass.]
> Mendoza: Can we offer you anything? Broiled rabbit and prickly pears--

BRIGAND'S BROILED RABBIT

For a party of 4.
Preparation time: about 40 minutes.

Two 2 pound domesticated rabbits (fresh or frozen), cut in halves lengthwise
1/4 cup melted butter or margarine
1 cup beef stock

For the sauce:
2 tablespoons butter or margarine
1 large clove garlic, peeled and minced
2-3 scallions, minced (green and white parts)
2 tablespoons flour
1 cup beef stock
1 cup port wine
Salt and freshly ground black pepper, to taste

Preheat the broiler.

Wash the rabbit halves and blot dry with paper towels. Brush with the melted butter or margarine.

Apply vegetable shortening to a paper towel and very carefully grease the hot broiler rack. Place the rabbits on the rack and broil, turning 3-4 times and basting with the beef stock, about 20 minutes.

While the rabbits broil, make the sauce: Melt the butter or margarine in a large skillet over medium heat. Add the garlic and scallions and sauté about 5 minutes. Sprinkle with the flour and cook, stirring frequently, until the flour is golden, 3-4 minutes. Add the beef stock and port and cook, stirring frequently, until smooth. Stir in any unused basting stock.

When the rabbits are done, remove them from the broiler and let stand, reserving any juices in the broiler pan and scraping the pan to loosen any clinging bits. Add the pan juices, salt and pepper to the sauce. Drizzle the sauce over the rabbits. Serve with rice, a steamed vegetable and Parker House Rolls (page 20.)

THE MAN WHO CAME TO DINNER
By George S. Kaufman and Moss Hart
(1939)

Ostensibly a burlesque of the lecture tours of drama critic Alexander Woollcott, this fast-moving farce-comedy concentrates on a waspish curmudgeon, Sheridan Whiteside, who delights in tormenting both admirers and antagonists. Monte Woolley created the character on Broadway, but Woollcott himself, as well as both collaborators, played the role in summer theatres.

Having taken over the small-town Ohio home of the Stanleys in consequence of a fall in which he presumably broke a hip, Whiteside proceeds to tyrannize the household. At the end of Act I, Scene 1, he announces the luncheon menu to his guests -- three hand-cuffed convicts and their armed guards:

> We're having chicken livers tetrazzini. . . . I hope every little tummy is a-flutter with gastric juices. Serve the white wine with the fish, John, and close the doors. I dont want a lot of people prying on their betters.

You may now share their cuisine without the burden of their company, particularly "Henderson, the hatchet fiend. Always chopped 'em up in a salad bowl-- remember?"

SHERIDAN WHITESIDE'S CHICKEN LIVERS TETRAZZINI

For a party of 6 to 8.
Preparation time: about 1 hour, including baking.

3-5 tablespoons olive oil
1 pound chicken livers, coarsely chopped
12 ounces fresh mushrooms, stemmed and sliced
1/2 cup drained, pitted and sliced ripe olives
3-5 tablespoons dry white wine or Chinese rice wine
1 pound uncooked pasta (spaghetti broken into pieces, elbow macaroni, ziti or penne)
4 tablespoons butter or margarine
4 tablespoons unbleached flour
2 cups chicken stock
Salt and freshly ground black pepper, to taste
$1^1/2$ cups heavy cream, whipping cream or light cream
Romano or Parmesan cheese, freshly grated

Preheat the oven to 375° F.

Cook the pasta *al dente*, according to package directions. Drain and set aside.

Heat a large skillet over moderately high heat and add 2 tablespoons of the olive oil. When the oil is hot, add the chicken livers and sauté gently to brown on all sides, about 5 minutes. Remove the livers from the pan with a slotted spoon and drain on paper towels.

Place the mushrooms in the skillet and sauté over moderately high heat, adding more oil as needed. When the mushrooms are golden and most of the moisture has cooked away, add the olives and stir once or twice. Add the wine to the skillet. When the wine begins to simmer, remove the skillet from the heat.

In a saucepan over medium-low heat, blend the butter and flour to make a smooth paste (roux). Add the chicken stock, a few tablespoons at a time, blending thoroughly after each addition. Remove the saucepan from the heat.

Warm the cream in a small saucepan over medium-high heat and stir into the stock mixture.

Combine the pasta and the mushroom mixture and toss to mix well. Add half the stock mixture and toss again-- carefully, to avoid splattering. Season with salt and pepper.

Place the chicken livers in a bowl and add the other half of the stock mixture, mixing gently to coat the livers. Season with salt and pepper. Place the pasta-mushroom mixture in a baking dish that has been sprayed with non-stick spray. Spread the liver mixture evenly over the pasta. Generously top with the cheese.

Bake in the middle of the oven until lightly browned and heated through, about 30 minutes.

Serve Sheridan Whiteside's Chicken Livers Tetrazzini with a garden salad, warm Italian bread and a robust red wine.

Whiteside promises that the dish will be followed by cherries jubilee. An excellent suggestion. A recipe is on page 38.

THE MARRIAGE
OF BETTE AND BOO
By Christopher Durang
(1985)

Durang's gift for parady of American life and his Absurdist approach to theatrical form have made him popular with regional and university theatre audiences. He can be devastating as well as very funny, although the topicality of his subject matter has kept his name from becoming a household word. In *The Marriage of Bette and Boo* he disects contemporary Catholic family life in thirty-three scenes.

In Scene 18, the climax of Act I, Bette (pronounced "Bet") and Boo invite their families to celebrate Thanksgiving. After some customary bickering in which Bette warns Boo: "Don't criticize my mother," her sister Joan enters carrying a serving dish with sweet potatoes. Another sister, Emily, holds a large gravy boat which unfortunately disrupts the scene when Boo drops the dish and attempts to clean up the gravy with a vacuum cleaner. In the chaos, the sweet potatoes are never eaten, a result we consider a serious flaw in Durang's consideration for actors.

CANDIED SWEET POTATOES

For a party of 6.
Preparation time: about 50 minutes, including baking.

1 tablespoon fresh lemon juice
5-6 large sweet potatoes
3/4 cup packed light brown sugar
1/2 teaspoon cinnamon
1/8 teaspoon nutmeg
2 tablespoons butter or margarine
Zest of 2 lemons, grated
2 tablespoons raisins

In a large pot, place several cups of cold water and add the lemon juice. Peel one potato at a time and cut lengthwise into 1/2" slices. As soon as the chunks are cut, drop them into the water. When all the potatoes have been added to the pot, add enough water to cover. Turn the heat to high and bring to a boil. Reduce heat to medium (just high enough to maintain a gentle boil) and cook until the potatoes are tender, about 15 minutes.

While the potatoes cook, preheat the oven to 375° F.

Drain the potatoes and discard the cooking water. Arrange the potatoes evenly in a large baking dish that has been sprayed with non-stick spray. Sprinkle with the brown sugar, cinnamon and nutmeg. Dot with the butter or margarine and top with the lemon zest and raisins. Place in the middle of the oven and bake until glazed, about 20 minutes. Serve hot.

♤ ♤ ♤ ♤ ♤

To contribute to the feast Bette's father and mother have brought "a large cake," which is mentioned only in the stage directions. Our apple cake does not appear to be very large, but it will feed a great many.

A LARGE APPLE CAKE

For a party of 10-12.
Preparation time: about 2 hours, including baking.

2 cups sugar
$1^1/2$ cups canola oil or safflour oil
2 eggs or 4 ounces egg substitute, beaten
3 cups unbleached flour
1/2 teaspoon salt
1 teaspoon baking soda
1 teaspoon cinnamon
1/2 teaspoon nutmeg
3 cups chopped apples
1 cup chopped walnuts
2 teaspoons vanilla

Preheat the oven to 350° F.

In a large bowl, mix together the sugar and oil. Add the eggs and stir until blended. In another large bowl, combine the flour, salt, baking soda, cinnamon and nutmeg. Add to the sugar mixture and stir with a sturdy wooden spoon (we've lost several to this cake!) until blended. Add the apples, walnuts and vanilla and continue stirring to mix well. The mixture will be very stiff. Spoon the mixture into a greased and floured 10" tube pan. Place in the middle of the oven and bake for about 1 hour and 25 minutes. Remove from the oven and allow to cool completely in the pan, on a wire rack, before removing from the pan.

Serve the cake at any temperature you wish. Top with a cream cheese frosting (triple the recipe for filling on page 28), if it pleases you.

（☆（☆（☆（☆（☆（☆（☆（☆

THE MATCHMAKER
By Thornton Wilder
(1954)

As a remake of Wilder's *Merchant of Yonkers* (1938), this play opened in London in 1954, came to New York the next year and gained even greater popularity when adapted by Michael Stewart as the musical *Hello, Dolly!* (1964), starring Carol Channing as Dolly Levi.

Mrs. Levi, the Matchmaker, has set her cap for Horace Vandergelder, the merchant. Act III, in the Harmonia Garden Restaurant, the Battery, New York, is typical of the play's farcical activity. Dining with Mrs. Levi, Vandergelder orders: "A chicken! A chicken like everybody else has," and a bottle of wine!

Complications arise when Vandergelder discovers that he has lost his purse ("Stop eating the chicken," he exclaims; "I can't pay for it!") and becomes enraged upon discovering his niece in the restaurant and his own clerks having an uproarious party at his expense at the next table.

> Mrs. Levi: Well, there's your life, Mr. Vandergelder! Without niece -- without clerks -- without bride -- and without your purse. Will you marry me now?
> Vandergelder: No!
> Mrs. Levi (to the audience): Damn!

CHICKEN LIKE EVERYBODY ELSE HAS

For a party of 4.

Preparation time: about 1 hour and 10 minutes, including simmering.

This is the first entrée we learned to cook as newlyweds, and, simple as it is, we still find it a delicious lifesaver today.

1 tablespoon butter or margarine
1 tablespoon flour
1 chicken fryer, skin and giblets removed, cut into pieces
1 can cream of chicken soup, undiluted
1 cup milk
Salt and freshly ground black pepper, to taste

In the bottom of a skillet large enough to hold the chicken pieces, blend the butter or margarine and flour to make a smooth paste (roux). Turn the heat to low to melt the butter. Spread the roux around the bottom of the skillet to cover completely. On top of the roux, spread about 3 tablespoons of the soup. Arrange the chicken pieces on top of the soup.

Blend the remaining soup with the milk until smooth and pour over the chicken. If the chicken is in more than a single layer, spoon some of the soup mixture between the pieces. Make sure all pieces of chicken are covered with the soup mixture. Bring to a simmer over high heat. Reduce heat to simmer, cover and cook, turning and basting occasionally, making sure the chicken does not stick to the skillet, until chicken is tender and the soup has thickened to the desired consistency, about 1 hour. Season with salt and pepper.

Serve Chicken Like Everybody Else Has (doesn't everybody have a can of chicken soup in the pantry?) with potatoes (mashed with butter or gravy, fried-- French or homestyle, or baked with butter and/or sour cream and/or chives?), tossed salad (with Thousand Island, French or Bleu Cheese dressing?), bread (white, whole wheat or rye?) and coffee (black or with cream and/or sugar or artificial sweetener?) or iced tea (with sugar and/or lemon?) and a bottle of New York State wine (red or white, dry or sweet?) -- just like everybody else has!

THE MEMBER OF THE WEDDING
By Carson McCullers
(1950)

Dramatizing her novel, first published in 1946, McCullers traces the maturing of adolescent Frankie Addams, reacting to the marriage of an older brother. Frankie's petulant yet irresistible self-centered innocence almost taxes the monumental good sense and patience of the family cook Berenice, played by Ethel Waters. Julie Harris played the role of Frankie and Brandon de Wilde the little boy next door.

Much of the action takes place in the kitchen, where early in Act II Berenice is making cookies, creaming butter and sugar for the kind of cookies that appeal to young Frankie and to all of us.

BERENICE'S COOKIE MAN COOKIES

About 3 dozen large cookies.
Preparation time: about 40 minutes, including baking.

1 cup granulated sugar
1/2 cup packed light brown sugar
3/4 cup butter or stick margarine
1 teaspoon vanilla extract
2 eggs or 4 ounces egg substitute
2 cups unbleached flour
1 teaspoon baking soda
A pinch of salt
1/2 cup peanut butter chips
$1^1/2$ cups chocolate chips

Preheat the oven to 350° F.

In a large bowl, mix the sugar and brown sugar and cream with the butter or margarine. Add the vanilla and blend well. Add the eggs or egg substitute and beat well.

In a separate bowl, combine the flour, baking soda and salt. Add the flour mixture to the sugar mixture, blending well.

Add the chips, about 1/2 cup at a time, stirring after each addition to distribute evenly.

Bake in batches of 12-15 cookies each: Place the mixture, by tablespoons, on an ungreased cookie sheet. Bake in the middle of the oven 10-12 minutes per batch, or until lightly browned.

Remove from the oven and let stand about 5 minutes. With a spatula, remove the cookies from the sheet to wire racks. Allow the cookies to cool completely (if you have Berenice's incredible strength of character) and serve with vanilla ice cream and coffee.

♪♫♪♫♪♪♫

In Act I we hear Sis Laura's voice as she peddles her vegetables from door to door: "Lots of okra, peas, fresh butter beans . . ." When, in Act II, news comes that Sis Laura has died of a stroke, Berenice is shocked: "Why she was by here just yesterday. We just ate her peas. They in my stomach right now, and her lyin' dead on the cooling board this minute. The Lord works in strange ways."

SIS LAURA'S PEA SALAD

Side dish for a party of 6.
Preparation time: about 10 minutes, plus $1^1/2$ hours precooking and cooling and, if chilling, 1-2 hours.

1 to $1^1/2$ tablespoons olive oil
1/2 cup cut scallions, whites only, in 1/4" rounds
3 cups fresh green peas
1-2 tablespoons mayonnaise
3/4 cup 1/4" cubes sharp cheddar cheese
1-2 tablespoons drained capers
1-2 tablespoons minced fresh ginger root
Salt and freshly ground black pepper, to taste

Place the green peas in a large saucepan, cover with water and bring to a boil over high heat.

Immediately reduce heat to simmer and cook until the peas are tender, about 30 minutes. Drain well and allow to cool at least 1 hour.

Heat a small skillet over medium heat and add the oil. When the oil is hot, add the scallions and sauté about 3 minutes. Remove the scallions from the skillet and drain on paper towels.

In a large bowl, combine the peas and mayonnaise and gently toss to coat. Add the onions, cheese, capers, ginger root and salt and pepper. Gently toss again. Serve at room temperature or well chilled. To enjoy a Southern-style meal, serve Sis Laura's Pea Salad with fried chicken (page 57), mashed potatoes and cream gravy, Parker House Rolls (page 20) or bisquits (page 127) and sweet iced tea. For dessert, serve Berenice's Cookie Man Cookies.

THE MIRACLE WORKER
By William Gibson
(1959)

This powerful play, depicting the struggle between an inexperienced but determined Annie Sullivan (played by Anne Bancroft) and a stubborn young Helen Keller (played by Patty Duke), enjoyed a lengthy initial run on Broadway.

Opening Act II, Annie writes to a friend that "the greatest problem I have is how to discipline her without breaking her spirit." In this act and later, food assumes an important role in Annie's struggle. At Breakfast in Act II, Helen, as usual, gropes through the plates of all present, fingering the bisquits, scrambled eggs and bacon. When she reaches Annie's plate, "Annie firmly pins her by the wrist and removes her hand from the table." And the confrontation begins. Later, in Act III, another crisis occurs at the dinner table, as Annie insists upon the table manners she has taught Helen.

The Miracle Worker is an extremely emotional play. Some soothing scrambled eggs might be welcome (if so, a recipe is on page 145), along with fresh, warm bisquits and coffee.

BREAKFAST BISQUITS

For a party of 4-6.
Preparation time: about 20 minutes, including baking.

3/4 cup milk
1 tablespoon white wine vinegar
2 cups unbleached flour, plus extra flour for dusting
2 teaspoons baking powder
1 teaspoon baking soda
1/2 teaspoon (or less) salt
5 tablespoons butter or margarine

Preheat the oven to 450° F.

In a small bowl, combine the milk and vinegar and let stand. Into a large bowl, sift together the flour, baking powder, baking soda and salt. Cut in the butter or margarine, using a pastry cutter or two knives. Pour in the milk and stir quickly. The dough will form a sticky mass. Working quickly, turn out the dough on a well-floured surface and pat into a 3/4" thickness. With a biscuit or cookie cutter, cut 8-10 circles and place on an ungreased baking sheet. Bake in the middle of the oven until golden, about 12 minutes.

Serve hot, with butter or margarine and honey.

MOTHER COURAGE
AND HER CHILDREN
By Bertolt Brecht
(1938)

Despite Brecht's theories of alienation and his view of the drama as purely a process for exploring the problems of the world, Mother Courage arouses feelings of admiration and sympathy in audiences. The play focuses upon the trading activities of Anna Fierling during the Thirty Years' War and the deaths of her three children.

In the second scene of the play, Mother Courage is trying to sell a capon to the cook of the Swedish Commander. She is a clever bargainer and finally gets a gilder for the foul, after she learns that her son is eating with the Commander. Mother Courage must pluck the capon; we hope you will spare yourself that part of the process -- and the bargaining as well-- by finding a juicy foul in your neighborhood market.

A COURAGEOUS COCQ

For a party of 8-10.
Preparation time: about 2 hours and 45 minutes, including simmering.

1 capon or large chicken (5-6 pounds)
1/2 lime
1/2 orange

2 tablespoons extra virgin olive oil
1 tablespoon butter or margarine
3-4 ounces slab bacon or salt pork
1-2 sprigs fresh thyme
1-2 sprigs fresh parsley
1 bay leaf
1 garlic clove, peeled and halved
8-10 whole black peppercorns
1 head cabbage, cut into small wedges
4-6 new potatoes, quartered
2-3 carrots, scraped and cut into 3/4" rounds
2-3 small turnips, peeled and cut in 1" chunks
2 onions, each studded with 2-4 whole cloves
2 ribs celery, cut into 3/4" slices
2 leeks, washed and cut in chunks (white part only)
Salt, freshly ground black pepper and cayenne or
    dried red pepper flakes, to taste

Remove the giblets from the capon. Wash the capon in cold water and pat dry, inside and out, with paper towels. Truss the capon as if for oven roasting (neck and lower cavities closed with skewers, wings and legs tied closely to the body). Rub the capon with the cut side of the lime, then with the cut side of the orange. Let stand a few minutes.

Make a bouquet garni: Wrap the thyme, parsley, bay leaf, garlic and peppercorns in a double thickness of cheesecloth and tie the ends to make a small pouch.

In a pot large enough to hold the capon comfortably, heat the oil and butter or margarine over moderately high heat. Add the capon and cook, turning to brown evenly, about 10-12 minutes. When the capon is browned, add the bacon or pork, bouquet garni and enough cold water to cover the capon. Bring to a boil over high heat. Immediately reduce heat to simmer and cook, skimming off any foam that forms on the surface, 30 minutes. Add the vegetables, salt and peppers. Raise heat to high and bring to a boil. Cover and cook, skimming as necessary, until the vegetables are tender, about 30 minutes. Drain all, reserving the liquid for another use. Discard the bouquet garni. Place the capon and vegetables on a warmed serving platter and carve at the table.

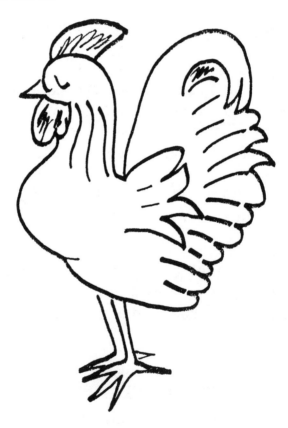

THE ODD COUPLE
By Neil Simon
(1965)

One of Simon's best loved comedies, *The Odd Couple* became a successful movie and was expanded into a popular television series.

When Felix Ungar's marriage breaks up, he moves into the Manhattan apartment of his friend, sportswriter Oscar Madison. But the alliance is an unholy one: Oscar is a determined slob; Felix is as fussy as a schoolmarm.

At one point, Felix has cooked a dish of linguine which Oscar insists on calling spaghetti. Felix, typically, corrects him. "It's linguine," he says. Oscar's none too abundant patience deserts him completely; he throws the pasta at the wall, where it sticks. "Now," he says, "it's garbage."

FELIX UNGAR'S LINGUINE

For a party of 8-10.
Preparation time: about 2 hours, including simmering.

1 tablespoon extra virgin olive oil
1 medium onion, finely chopped
2 cloves garlic, peeled and minced
1 cup sliced fresh mushrooms
1 cup chopped sweet red bell pepper

1 can (28 ounces) crushed tomatoes in tomato purée
1/4 teaspoon sugar
6 ounces tomato paste
$1^1/2$ cups dry white wine
2 bay leaves
2 teaspoons dried basil
1 teaspoon dried red pepper flakes
1/2 cup chopped fresh parsley or Italian parsley
Salt and freshly ground black pepper, to taste
$1^1/2$ pounds uncooked linguine noodles
Romano or Parmesan cheese, freshly grated, for
   topping

Heat a large skillet over moderately high heat and add the oil. When the oil is hot, add the onion and sauté, stirring occasionally, until translucent, about 3-4 minutes. Stir in the garlic and sauté about 1 minute. Reduce heat to low, add the bell pepper and mushrooms and sauté about 3 minutes. Add 1/2 cup of the crushed tomatoes, the sugar and tomato paste. Cook, stirring occasionally, about 10 minutes. Add the remaining tomatoes, the wine, bay leaves, basil, red pepper flakes, parsley and salt and pepper. Simmer, uncovered, at least 1 hour (the longer it simmers, the better it will taste).

While the sauce simmers, cook the linguine *al dente*, according to package directions. (Pasta cooked *al dente* may not stick to the wall, but it will be more pleasing to your palate.)

Just before serving, discard the bay leaves from the tomato sauce.

Place the linguine on a warm serving platter or on individual warm plates, top generously with the sauce and cheese. Serve with a leafy green salad and crusty Italian or garlic bread.

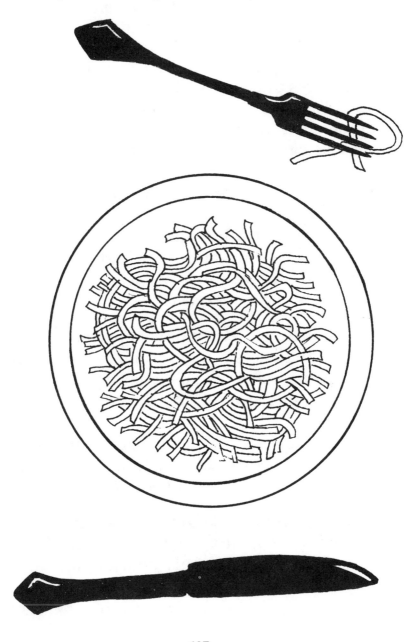

THE OLD HOMESTEAD
By Denman Thompson
(1886)

The best example of local color melodrama of New England, this play started in 1875 as a sketch called *Joshua Whitcomb*. Under its present title its success is unmatched in America. Thompson played the major role every year until his death in 1911; other actors took over the part of Uncle Josh; at least five film versions have been made. The scene of the play is Swansea, New Hampshire (just outside Keene), where each July modern theatregoers may visit the Potash Bowl and laugh and cry as the Old Homestead Association of Swansea produces Thompson's masterpiece.

The plot includes everything nineteenth century American audiences wanted: country humor, moral observations, city versus country conflicts, a temperance theme, a returning prodigal, and more. Uncle Josh filled the theatre with sentiment as he gave the curtain speech: "Come up in June when all natur' is at her best -- come on, all of you, and let the scarlet runners chase you back to childhood."

In Act I, as Aunt Tilda gets supper in a kitchen described in realistic detail, the meal is not described, but it could only be a traditional New Hampshire boiled dinner.

A NEW HAMPSHIRE BOILED DINNER

For a party of 8-10.
Preparation time: about 3 hours, including simmering.

3 pounds beef brisket or corned beef
8-10 small beets, tops removed
5-6 carrots, scraped and cut into 1" chunks
3-4 small turnips, peeled and cut into 1" cubes
6 medium potatoes, cut into $1^1/2$" cubes
8-10 small onions, peeled
1 small head cabbage, cut into 8-10 wedges
Salt and freshly ground black pepper, to taste

Place the beef in a large pot and cover with cold water. Bring to a boil over high heat, skimming off any foam that forms on the surface. Reduce heat to simmer and cover. Cook until the beef is tender, about 2 $^1/2$ hours.

While the beef simmers, place the beets in a saucepan and half cover them with boiling water. Reduce heat to simmer, cover and cook until tender, about 40 minutes for young beets, up to 2 hours for older beets. Drain, cool slightly and slip off and discard the skins. Keep the beets warm. To the beef pot add the carrots, turnips, potatoes and onions. Simmer 15 minutes. Add the cabbage and simmer 15 minutes more, or until all the vegetables are tender. Add the salt and pepper.

Drain the beef and vegetables and place the beef in the center of a warm serving platter. Surround the beef with the vegetables, including the beets.

OUR TOWN
By Thornton Wilder
(1938)

America's favorite play! Even the caustic drama critic Alexander Woolcott had to admit that "no play ever moved me so deeply." The Stage Manager in "our town" (Grover's Corners, New Hampshire) says: "The cottage, the go-cart, the Sunday afternoon drive in the Ford, the first rheumatism, the grandchildren, the second rheumatism, the death bed, the reading of the will.-- Once in a thousand times it's interesting." But few can resist the fascinating simplicity of Wilder's ideas: "Let's look at one another!" Emily pleads. And we still try.

The title of Act II is "Love and Marriage." The time is July 7, 1904. Dr. and Mrs. Gibbs, George's folks, talk of their own wedding as they get ready for George and Emily's Big Day.

> Dr. Gibbs: There I was in the Congregational Church marryin' a total stranger.
>
> Mrs. Gibbs: And how do you think I felt! Frank, weddings are perfectly awful things. Farces, -- that's what they are! (She puts a plate before him.)   Here, I've made something for you.
>
> Dr. Gibbs: Why Julia Hersey -- French toast!
>
> Mrs. Gibbs: 'Taint hard to make and I had to do <u>some</u>thing.

Our Town is every town, and we all know that feeling. And she's right, "'taint hard to make."

MRS. GIBBS' WEDDING DAY FRENCH TOAST

For a party of 6-8.
Preparation time: about 30 minutes.

Enough loaves of fresh Italian or French bread to
    make 16-18 slices 3/4" thick
9-10 eggs or 20 ounces egg substitute, lightly beaten
1 cup light cream, half and half or milk
Salt and freshly ground black pepper, to taste
Canola oil or safflour oil

Place the oven on the "warm" setting.

Cut the bread diagonally into slices about 3/4" thick.

In a mixing bowl, combine the eggs, cream or milk and salt and pepper. Transfer the mixture to a large, flat-bottomed bowl or pan. Lay the slices of bread, in batches, in a single layer in the bowl or pan. Allow the bread to soak about 30 seconds on one side, turn and soak about 30 seconds on the other side. Tilt the slices upward to coat the edges.

As the bread will cook in batches, you may want to cook one batch while the next one soaks.

Heat a large skillet and add enough oil to cover the bottom. When the oil is hot, begin to add the bread slices, in a single layer. Cook the bread over moderately high heat, turning as needed, until golden brown on both sides and slightly crisp around the edges. Add additional oil as needed.

As you remove the bread from the skillet, stack the slices on an oven-proof plate and place them in the oven to keep warm. When all the slices are cooked, serve immediately with butter or margarine and maple syrup or a sprinkling of sugar and freshly grated nutmeg.

THE PHILADELPHIA STORY
By Philip Barry
(1939)

A critic once described Barry as "the lightning bug-- now he lights up, now he doesn't." With *The Philadelphia Story* Barry lit up Broadway for a year. Katharine Hepburn scored a great success as Tracy Lord, the socialite, along with Shirley Booth and Joseph Cotten.

What do the aristocrats living on the Main Line outside Philadelphia eat for breakfast? In Act III, they eat hotcakes and bacon. Here is our version-- and you do not need to be a millionaire!

HOTCAKES PHILADELPHIA

For a party of 4.
Preparation time: about 15 minutes.

1^1/4 cups unbleached flour
2 teaspoons baking powder
1/2 teaspoon (or less) salt
2 tablespoons sugar
1 egg white
1 cup milk
2 tablespoons butter or margarine, melted

In a medium mixing bowl, combine the flour, baking powder, salt and sugar. In a large bowl, lightly whisk the egg white. Add the milk and whisk to blend. Add the melted butter or margarine and whisk again. Add the flour mixture and stir with a fork just until the dry ingredients are moistened. The batter will be slightly lumpy.

Lightly oil a well-seasoned griddle or skillet and heat over moderately high heat. For each hotcake, pour a scant 1/4 cup batter onto the griddle or skillet. Cook, turning once, until golden on both sides.

Serve with butter or margarine and syrup or sugar and nutmeg. And, of course, crisp bacon!

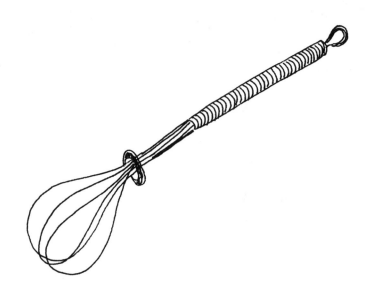

≋≋≋≋≋≋≋≋≋≋≋≋≋≋≋≋≋≋≋≋≋≋≋≋≋≋≋≋≋≋

THE RAINMAKER
By N. Richard Nash
(1954)

This popular romantic comedy set in a western state during a summer drought has been translated into thirty languages, made into a movie and revived as a musical (*110 in the Shade*, 1964).

Toward the end of Act I in the Curry home, Lizzie (a role created on stage by Geraldine Page) is finishing supper preparations. She is excited about a guest for the meal and warns her brother: "Now don't walk heavy because the lemon cake will fall!" It is, we are told, "the prettiest lemon cake" she could imagine.

LIZZIE'S LEMON CAKE

For a party of 10-12 (Makes a 2-layer cake, 8" round).
Preparation time: about 3 hours, including baking and cooling.

2/3 cup butter or margarine, softened
$1^1/3$ cups sifted granulated sugar
Zest of 1 large lemon, grated
$2\,^1/3$ cups sifted cake flour
$2\,^1/2$ teaspoons double-acting baking powder
1/8 teaspoon salt
2/3 cup milk

1/2 teaspoon vanilla extract
5-6 egg whites

For the frosting:
2 ounces cream cheese, softened
3/4 cup butter or margarine, softened
1 pound confectioners sugar
1 teaspoon vanilla
Zest of 1/2 large lemon, grated

Bring all the ingredients to room temperature. Preheat the oven to 350° F.

In a large bowl, cream the butter or margarine, sugar and lemon zest until light and fluffy.

In another bowl, resift the flour twice with the baking powder and salt. Add the flour mixture to the butter mixture in 3 parts, alternately with the milk, beginning and ending with flour and stirring until smooth after each addition. Stir in the vanilla.

In another bowl, whip the egg whites until stiff but not dry. Gently fold the egg whites into the cake batter. Pour the batter in equal parts into 2 greased and floured 8" round cake pans. Bake about 35-40 minutes or until a toothpick inserted in the center of the cake comes out clean. Remove the cake from the oven and cool in the pans on wire racks about 5 minutes. Remove from the pans and cool completely on the racks before frosting.

Make the frosting: In a large bowl, cream together the cream cheese and butter or margarine. Add the confectioners sugar gradually, creaming until the mixture is completely blended and smooth. Add the vanilla and lemon zest and blend thoroughly. (You may use an electric mixer to blend all the ingredients.) Cover with plastic wrap and refrigerate until ready to use.

A RAISIN IN THE SUN
By Lorraine Hansberry
(1959)

The first play on Broadway by a Black woman, *A Raisin in the Sun* won the New York Drama Critics Circle Award. A number of Black performers profitted from its long run: Ruby Dee, Sidney Poitier, Diana Sands and Lonne Elder III.

In the first scene of the play, Ruth Younger asks her husband, Walter Lee, how he wants his eggs cooked. "Not scrambled," he replies. But she proceeds to scramble the eggs anyway, and the day begins.

> Walter: That's it. There you are. Man say to his woman: "I got me a dream." His woman say: "Eat your eggs." Man say: "I got to take hold of this here world, baby!" And his woman say: "--Your eggs is getting cold!"
> [A few moments pass.]
> Ruth: Eat your eggs, Walter.
> Walter: Damn my eggs . . . damn all the eggs that ever was!

Damned or not, these eggs are good!

WALTER'S SCRAMBLED EGGS

For a party of 6.
Preparation time: about 5-7 minutes.

1 dozen large eggs, brown or white
1 cup half and half or milk
Salt and freshly ground black pepper, to taste
Canola oil or safflour oil

Break the eggs into a large bowl and add the cream or milk and salt and pepper. Beat lightly with a wire whisk.

Heat a large skillet over medium heat and add enough oil to cover the bottom. (The eggs will have a richer flavor, and more fat, if you melt a little butter in the heated oil before adding the eggs.) When the oil is hot, pour in the egg mixture, all at once. When the eggs touching the bottom of the skillet turn white and begin to cook, begin to stir with a small spatula (we use a wooden wok paddle), scraping the bottom of the skillet to prevent sticking and over cooking. (The more vigorously you stir, the more slowly the eggs will cook and the less fluffy they will be when done. For fluffier eggs, use fewer but larger strokes.)

When eggs are fluffy and slightly moist, remove from heat and transfer to a heated serving bowl. Serve immediately with bisquits (page 127) or toast wedges, fruit juice and coffee.

RIP VAN WINKLE
Created by Dion Boucicault
and Joseph Jefferson
(1865)

The story of Rip Van Winkle comes from *The Sketch Book* (1819) of Washington Irving, but the play is closely associated with the actor Joseph Jefferson, who wrote in 1881 that he had acted the title role about 2,500 times and subsequently continued to do so until his death in 1905. For contemporary audiences he *was* Rip Van Winkle, and he embellished the part to suit his acting style.

A lovable ne'er-do-well, Rip is at his best drinking and telling stories with his friends. To his long-suffering wife, Gretchen, he is a poor provider and a teaser.

In Act II, returning home with his gun, Rip describes his encounter with a rabbit.

>Gretchen: I like rabbit. I like it in a stew.
>Rip: I guess you like everything in a stew-- everything what's a rabbit, I swear. Well, there was a rabbit a feedin' mit the grass -- you know they always come out early in der morning and feed mit the grass.
>Gretchen: Never mind the grass. Go on.
>Rip: Don't get so patient; you wait till you get the rabbit. Well I crawl up--

Gretchen: Yes, yes.

Rip: An' his little tail was a-stickin' up so--
(business)

Gretchen: Never mind his tail. Go on.

Rip: The more fatter the rabbit, the more whiter
is his tail--

Gretchen: Well, well, go on.

Rip (taking aim): Well, I haul up--

Gretchen: Yes, yes!

Rip: And his ears was a-stickin' up so--
(business)

Gretchen: Never mind his ears. Go on.

Rip: I pull the trigger.

Gretchen: Bang went the gun, and--

Rip: And the rabbit run away.

Here is a recipe featuring a rabbit that did not run away.

RIP 'S RABBIT STEW

For a party of 8.

Preparation time: about 3 hours and 15 minutes, including simmering.

2 domesticated rabbits (fresh or frozen), about 2
    pounds each
1/2 cup unbleached flour
2 tablespoons butter or margarine
1 tablespoon olive oil
3 medium onions, minced
2 cloves garlic, peeled and minced
1 can (28 ounces) crushed tomatoes in tomato purée
1 can (6 ounces) tomato paste
1-2 bay leaves
2 Irish potatoes, skins on, cut into 1" cubes
3-4 carrots, cut into 3/4" rings
1 cup green peas (fresh or frozen)
1 cup cleaned, stemmed and sliced fresh
    mushrooms
Salt and freshly ground black pepper, to taste
Dried red pepper flakes, to taste
1 tablespoon Worcestershire sauce
1 cup red wine
Chicken stock, for thinning

Place the rabbit pieces and the flour in a paper or plastic bag and shake to coat evenly.

In a large hot skillet, melt and blend the butter or margarine and olive oil. Arrange the rabbit pieces in a single layer in the skillet and brown over moderately high heat, turning until browned on all sides. If your skillet will not hold all the pieces, brown them in batches, adding more butter or margarine and oil as needed. When evenly browned, remove the rabbit from the skillet and set aside.

Reduce heat to medium and add the onions and garlic to the skillet. Cook until the onions are translucent.

Place the rabbit, onions and garlic in a large pot. Add the tomatoes and their purée, the tomato paste and bay leaves and enough water to cover the rabbit. Bring to a boil, skimming off foam as it forms. Reduce heat and simmer until the rabbit is tender when tested with a fork, about 2 hours.

Add the potatoes, carrots, peas and mushrooms. Season with the salt, pepper and red pepper flakes. Add the Worcester sauce and wine. Return to a boil, reduce heat, cover and simmer until the meat pulls easily from the bone and the vegetables are cooked to the desired tenderness.

If the stew liquid is too thick, add some hot chicken stock. To thicken, use a baster to remove several cups of the liquid to a saucepan, cook over high heat to reduce, return the thickened liquid to the stew and stir to blend. Remove the pieces of rabbit from the stew. Carefully (there are many small bones!) remove the meat from the bones, discarding the bones and returning the meat to the stew.

Serve Rip's Rabbit Stew with crusty Italian bread or corn muffins.

THE RIVER NIGER
By Joseph A. Walker
(1972)

This thought-provoking play was performed by the Negro Ensemble Company before being transferred to Broadway in 1973. Without traditional division of scenes, it tells the story of a Harlem family yearning for substance and happiness in a world of hatred and love, death and innocence, sacrifice and violence.

Spending the night with the family, Ann Vanderguild from South Africa tries to make herself useful.

> Ann: I make a very good meat loaf, ma'am. I noticed you've got all the ingredients as I was putting the food away.

ANN'S MEATLOAF

For a party of 8.
Preparation time: about 1 hour and 45 minutes, including baking.

1 pound lean ground beef
1 pound lean ground pork
1/2 pound ground white meat of turkey
1 medium onion, peeled and finely chopped
1 large clove garlic, peeled and minced

1 egg white
1 tablespoon Worcestershire sauce
1/2 cup finely minced parsley
1 teaspoon ground basil
1/2 cup very finely crushed cracker crumbs
Salt and freshly ground black pepper, to taste

For the sauce:
1 cup beef stock
1 tablespoon butter or margarine
1 tablespoon flour
1/2 cup sliced fresh mushroom caps
2-3 finely chopped scallions (green and white parts)
Salt and freshly ground black pepper, to taste

Preheat the oven to 375° F.

In a large bowl, combine the beef, pork and turkey and, using your hands, mix well. Add the onion and garlic and mix well. Lightly beat the egg white and stir into the meat mixture. Add the Worcestershire sauce, parsley, basil, bread crumbs and salt and pepper. Using your hands, mix the ingredients together until all are thoroughly combined. With wet hands, press the mixture into a greased loaf pan (about 8 $^1/_2$" x 4 $^1/_2$" x 2 $^1/_2$").

Place the meatloaf in the middle of the oven and cook about 1 hour and 10 minutes. Remove from oven and let stand in the pan 5 minutes. Remove the meatloaf from the pan and keep warm.

Make the sauce: Remove and discard any fat remaining in the loaf pan. Add about 1/2 cup beef stock to the loaf pan and stir and scrape to loosen any clinging bits. In a large skillet over medium heat, blend the butter or margarine and the flour to make a smooth paste (roux). Add the beef stock from the loaf pan and stir to blend. Add the mushrooms and scallions and cook, stirring constantly, about 2 minutes. Add the remaining stock, raise heat to moderately high and stir constantly until the sauce thickens. Season with the salt and pepper.

Place the meatloaf on a warm serving platter and slice. Drizzle the gravy over the slices and serve.

ＹＩ ＹＩ ＹＩ ＹＩ ＹＩ ＹＩ

Later, Mattie tells Ann: "Listen, honey, I got a roast in the oven. Take it out in twenty-five minutes exactly." A recipe for pot roast is on page 13.

And later still, Jeff, the family's son home from the Air Force, describes his ideal meal.

> Jeff: Knows what I wants for dinner? Some corn bread, yeah. And some of Grandma's mustard greens, Mama . . . and black-eyed peas. And some of your candied sweets, Grandma, with lemon and raisins all over 'em, yeah!

Jeff's favorites would be good with meatloaf or pot roast. A recipe for "candied sweets" is on page 116.

ΩΩΩΩΩΩΩΩΩΩΩΩΩΩΩΩΩ

SAME TIME, NEXT YEAR
By Bernard Slade
(1975)

A slight comedy about an adulterous tryst that is repeated annually for twenty-five years, *Same Time, Next Year* captured the public fancy in New York and ran for 1,453 performances.

How did it get started? We learn in Act I, Scene 7.

> Doris: It started when you sent me over that steak in the restaurant.
> George: They didn't serve drinks. Steak was all they had.
> Doris: What made you think I was a medium rare?
> George: I'm very intuitive.

If you want to get something started -- an evening which includes the theatre, perhaps -- we suggest the following:

INTUITIVE BROILED STEAK

For a party of 6.
Preparation time: about 10 minutes.

6 Porterhouse, sirloin, strip or T-bone steaks, $1^1/2$"-2" thick

About 1 hour before cooking, remove the steaks from the refrigerator.

Preheat the broiler.

Place the steaks on a broiling grid over a shallow broiling pan, both of which have been sprayed with non-stick spray. If the steaks are $1^1/2$" thick, place them 3" from the heat source and broil, turning once, about 7 minutes on each side for rare, about 8 minutes on each side for medium. If steaks are 2" thick, place them 4" from the heat source and broil about 9 minutes per side for rare and 10 minutes per side for medium.

Spread the steaks with butter, margarine or pan drippings and serve with Texas toast (thick-sliced bread pan-fried in hot butter or margarine), a tossed green salad, sautéed mushrooms and the traditional middle-American favorite -- baked potatoes. Or, for a more sophisticated presentation, serve with Bordelaise à la Bordelaise (page 25), warm French bread, boiled new potatoes and steamed green beans.

SHAKUNTALA
By Kalidasa
(5th Century, A.D.)

As no one knows exactly when India's greatest poet and dramatist lived, we cannot date his best-known work. *Shakuntala* is basically different from western plays in that, like all Sanskrit drama, it subordinates plot and imitates a state of emotion. As King Dushyanta prays in the final lines of the play: "May Shiva see my faith on earth/And make me free of all rebirth."

By western standards, *Shakuntala* is a romantic melodrama. Having fallen in love with Shakuntala, King Dushyanta marries her before being called back to his kingdom. Upon his departure, he gives her a ring, "a token of remembrance" necessary to break the spell of forgetfulness cast on the king by a vengeful nymph. When Shakuntala loses the ring, she is rejected by the king, who does not recognize her.

In Act VI, a poor fisherman is arrested for trying to sell a ring he has found in the belly of a large carp. Dushyanta sees the ring and regains his memory, but Shakuntala has already left his kingdom.

Lest you worry, Sanskrit dramas always end happily, and we hope your experience with carp will do the same.

KALIDASA *MIN MAPPAS* (CARP)

For a party of 6.
Preparation time: about 30 minutes.

2 teaspoons coriander seed
1 teaspoon ground tumeric
8-10 black peppercorns
1/4 teaspoon dried red pepper flakes
1 teaspoon mustard seed
1 small (2") red onion, peeled and thinly sliced
2-3 cloves garlic, peeled and minced
2 tablespoons peanut oil
3/4 cup coconut milk
1 ripe mango, peeled and cut into 1" squares 1/4" thick
Salt, to taste
2 pounds carp (or other firm-fleshed white fish: cod, red snapper, halibut, haddock), cut into $1^1/2$" chunks

Toast the coriander, tumeric, peppercorns and 1/8 teaspoon of the red pepper flakes and grind with about 1 tablespoon water to make a paste.

Mix the mustard seed, onion, garlic and the remaining red pepper flakes. Heat a skillet over moderately high heat and add the oil. When the oil is hot, add the mustard mixture. Sauté 3 minutes. Add the ground spices and sauté 1 minute. Add 1 tablespoon water and cook until it evaporates. Add 1/2 cup of the coconut milk, the mango, salt and fish. Toss. Cook until the fish is done, about 8 minutes. Heat the remaining coconut milk and pour over the fish. Serve hot, with white rice.

SHE STOOPS TO CONQUER
By Oliver Goldsmith
(1773)

Historians tell us that Dr. Samuel Johnson sat in a side-box and laughed uproariously when this play was first performed. Horace Walpole, however, thought it "the lowest of all farces," and leading actors of the time refused major roles in it. You may hold your own views, but the play is still read and occasionally performed.

The most interesting references to food occur in Act II, Scene 1. Marlow and Hastings, enroute to the Hardcastle residence, are directed to this same house by the mischief-maker Tony Lumpkin, who tells them that it is a public inn. Expecting their arrival, Hardcastle treats them as guests and friends. They think him the landlord and demand a menu which they then arrogantly disparage.

> Marlowe (reading): For the first course at the top, a pig and prune sauce.
> Hastings: Damn your pig, I say.
> Marlowe: And damn your prune sauce, I say.
> Hardcastle: And yet, gentlemen, to men that are hungry, pig with prune sauce is very good eating.
> Marlowe: At the bottom, a calf's tongue and brains.
> Hastings: Let your brains be knocked out, my good sir; I don't like them.

Aghast at their impudence, Hardcastle struggles to remain polite while they make fun of the elaborate culinary preparations he has made for their arrival.

We can only regret the misunderstanding and the lost opportunities for the two young men. Since they rejected both the pig and the brains, we will offer a recipe for the remaining entrée.

TONGUE A` LA HARDCASTLE

For a party of 6-8.
Preparation time: about 5 hours, including soaking and simmering.

A 4 pound beef tongue*, roots removed
2 teaspoons (or less) salt
3/4 cup plus 2 tablespoons butter or margarine
4 medium carrots, scraped and cut into large chunks
2 medium onions, peeled and coarsely chopped
1 rib celery, coarsely chopped
4-5 ounces slab bacon or salt pork, cut into 1½" cubes
2 bay leaves
6-8 whole peppercorns
1 tablespoon flour
1 cup dry white wine
3 ¼ cups beef stock
2 veal bones
1 fresh horseradish root or parsley root
1 teaspoon dried thyme
2-3 sprigs fresh parsley
Salt and freshly ground black pepper, to taste

For the sauce:
1 tablespoon flour
2 tablespoons butter or margarine, softened
1 cup dry white wine
2 tablespoons (or more) cream-style horseradish

*We have substituted beef tongue for the calf's tongue of the play because beef tongue is usually preferable.

In a large bowl, soak the tongue in cold water about 2 hours. Drain and place in a large pot. Add 3 quarts cold water and the salt and bring to a boil. Cook, skimming off foam that forms on the surface, about 10 minutes. Drain and cool under cold running water until cool enough to handle. With a very sharp knife, scrape and peel off the thick outer skin, leaving the thin white film beneath it. Blot dry with paper towels. In a saucepan large enough to hold the tongue without forcing it, melt the butter or margarine over medium heat. Add the carrots, onions, celery and bacon or pork and cook until the vegetables begin to soften, about 3 minutes.

Tie the bay leaves and peppercorns in a small pouch made of a double thickness of cheesecloth. Place the tongue in the pot and cook, turning to brown evenly on all sides, about 10 minutes. Add the flour and turn and stir to distribute evenly. Stir in the wine, then the stock, veal bones, root, thyme, parsley and the cheesecloth pouch. The tongue should be about half covered by the liquid. Add salt and pepper and bring just to a boil. Reduce heat to low, cover and simmer about 2 hours, turning the tongue about every 40 minutes, skimming off any foam. Pierce the tongue with a metal cake tester; if the tester meets no resistance, the tongue is done. Place the tongue on a carving board, reserving the other contents of the pot.

Make the sauce: Remove and reserve the vegetables from the pot, discarding the other solids. Skim off and discard the fat from the surface of the liquid and reserve $1^1/2$ cups of the liquid. Press the vegetables through a sieve, or purée with a bit of the reserved liquid in a blender. In a bowl, combine the butter or margarine with the flour and blend to make a smooth paste (roux). In the pot over high heat, combine the reserved cooking liquid and the wine and bring to a boil. Quickly stir the roux into the boiling liquid. Add the vegetable purée and horseradish and cook, stirring constantly, until the sauce is smooth.

To slice the tongue, begin at the hump and work toward the tip. Slice vertically at first, slanting the cutting edge more and more toward the hump as you move forward, so that the final slices are virtually horizontal.

Stir any juices that come out of the tongue into the sauce. Place the tongue on a warm serving platter and drizzle sauce over the slices. Serve the extra sauce in a bowl. Serve with white rice or boiled new potatoes, a steamed or creamed vegetable and crusty bread.

Leftover tongue, served cold with Dijon mustard on rye bread, makes an excellent sandwich!

🌴 🌴 🌴 🌴 🌴 🌴 🌴 🌴 🌴 🌴 🌴 🌴 🌴 🌴 🌴 🌴 🌴 🌴 🌴 🌴

SOUTH PACIFIC
By Joshua Logan, Richard Rodgers
and Oscar Hammerstein, II
(1949)

Based on James Michener's novel, *Tales of the South Pacific*, this lavish musical starred Mary Martin as Nellie Forbush and Ezio Pinza as the romantic widowed Frenchman, Emile DeBecque.

> I'm as corny as Kansas in August [sings Nellie] ,
> I'm as normal as blueberry pie,
> No more a smart little girl with no heart,
> I have found me a wonderful guy.

But her wonderful guy has a secret in his past and two children by an island woman, and Nellie has prejudice in her upbringing. As the worldly planter and Army nurse from Little Rock fall in love, the authors find just the right words to express their feelings in such songs as "Wonderful Guy" and "Some Enchanted Evening." And Nellie has a chance to change her way of thinking -- when she discovers that Emile has volunteered for a hero's mission that endangers his life.

Critics still refer to *South Pacific* as Rodgers and Hammerstein's finest achievement, showing as it does the power of love to overcome fear and hatred in a war-torn world.

Let's eat to that!!!

NELLIE'S NORMAL BLUEBERRY PIE

For a party of 6-8.
Preparation time: about 1 hour, including baking.

For the filling:
3 pints fresh blueberries
1 cup sugar
2 tablespoons cornstarch
Zest of one lemon, grated

For the crust:
1/2 cup milk
1 teaspoon vinegar
1/2 cup vegetable shortening
1/2 cup margarine, softened
2 cups unbleached flour, plus extra flour for dusting
    and rolling
1 tablespoon sugar

Place the blueberries in a large bowl. Add the sugar and cornstarch and toss to coat evenly. Add 4 tablespoons water and the lemon zest and toss again. Set aside.

Make the crust: Preheat the oven to 425° F. In a small bowl, combine the milk and vinegar and set aside. In another small bowl, cream together the shortening and margarine. Place the flour in a large bowl. With a dough blender or 2 knives, cut in the shortening mixture. Add the milk and mix thoroughly with a wooden spoon. The dough will be very sticky. Liberally dusting your hands and the dough with flour, work the dough until you can form a ball. Divide the ball into 2 equal parts. On a well-floured surface, roll out one part in a circle for the bottom crust. When the circle is about 1/8" thick, press into a pie pan and trim, leaving an edge sufficient for attaching the upper crust.

Fill the bottom crust with the blueberry mixture. Roll out the top crust and place over the pie. Trim the edge. With a fork, join the crusts around the edge, pressing firmly. Prick the top crust several times with the fork to allow steam to escape during baking. Sprinkle the pie with the sugar and bake in the middle of the oven about 10 minutes. Reduce heat to 350° F. and bake until golden brown, about 20 minutes. Cool in the pan on a wire rack.

Serve Nellie's Normal Blueberry Pie warm, topped with vanilla ice cream.

A STREETCAR NAMED DESIRE
By Tennessee Williams
(1947)

Very early in the play Blanche explains: "They told me to take a street-car named Desire, and then transfer to one called Cemeteries and ride six blocks and get off at -- Elysian Fields!" With this foreshadowing, Williams continued his interest in neurotic conflicts and the loneliness of the human heart. Jessica Tandy played Blanche, Kim Hunter her sister, Stella, and Marlon Brando the "brute," Stanley. The play won a Pulitzer Prize.

In Scene 7, despite conflicts in the household, Stella prepares to celebrate Blanche's birthday with a white cake (page 27) with pink candles. Blanche's temporary happiness fades, however, when her new suitor does not appear. Scene 8 opens with Blanche, Stella and Stanley eating a birthday supper of chops at a table set for four.

NEW ORLEANS PORK CHOPS

For a party of 6.
Preparation time: about 1 hour and 40 minutes, including baking.

1/2 cup flour
6 center-cut pork chops, 3/4" thick, with excess fat
    removed
Olive oil, canola oil or safflour oil

1 large onion, finely chopped
2 large cloves garlic, peeled and minced
1 sweet red bell pepper, with membranes and seeds
    removed, thinly sliced
1/2 cup dry white wine
1/2 cup beef stock
1 cup canned crushed tomatoes in tomato purée
1/2 cup chopped celery
2 bay leaves
1/8 teaspoon sugar
1/2 teaspoon paprika
1/2 teaspoon dried red pepper flakes
Salt and freshly ground black pepper, to taste
1 cup coarsely crushed cornflakes

Preheat the oven to 350° F.

Place the flour in a plastic or paper bag. Add the chops, in batches if necessary, and shake the bag to coat the chops evenly with flour.

Heat a large skillet over moderately high heat and add enough oil to cover the bottom. Place the chops in the skillet in a single layer and cook until very slight blackening occurs on one side, about 5-6 minutes. Turn and cook until golden brown on the other side, about 4 minutes. Place the chops in a single layer in a baking dish that has been sprayed with non-stick spray. Set aside.

Remove and discard any fat from the skillet. Add enough oil just to cover the bottom. Add the onions (they will pick up the blackness from the chops) and sauté, stirring occasionally, over moderately high heat about 5 minutes. Add the garlic and red bell pepper and sauté about 1 minute. Add the wine and reduce heat to medium. Add the beef stock, tomatoes and their purée, celery, bay leaves, sugar, paprika, red pepper flakes and salt and pepper. Bring the liquid just to a simmer, then spoon over the chops, lifting each chop to allow liquid to cover the bottom of the baking dish.

Cover the baking dish with foil and bake in the middle of the oven about 1 hour. Top the chops with the cornflakes and bake, uncovered, about 15 minutes more. Remove the bay leaves.

Serve New Orleans Pork Chops with white rice or potatoes, steamed green beans or broccoli, and crusty bread or Parker House Rolls (page 20).

THE SUBJECT WAS ROSES
By Frank Gilroy
(1964)

Frequently revived by regional theatres, this play explores the problems of parents competing for the affections of a son just returned from war. It won all the major awards in 1964, but Gilroy has never been able to repeat his success.

In Act II, Scene 1, John and Nellie Cleary and their son Timmy are getting ready to go to Grandmother's house for dinner. They are expected at 12:00 noon. The meal will be ravioli and meat balls, and Grandmother's reputation as a cook suggests that one should not be tardy.

GRANDMOTHER'S RAVIOLI

For a party of 6.
Preparation time: 2-3$^1/2$ hours, depending upon resting time.

For the pasta:
1$^3/4$ cups unbleached flour
2 eggs
1/4 teaspoon (or less) salt

For the filling:
1 tablespoon extra virgin olive oil
1 small onion (about 2" diameter), finely minced

1-2 cloves garlic, peeled and finely minced
A 10 ounce package frozen spinach, thawed and
    drained
1 cup part-skim ricotta cheese
1/4 cup freshly grated Romano or Parmesan cheese
1/2 teaspoon dried basil
Salt and freshly ground black pepper, to taste
1 tablespoon olive oil

For the sauce:
3 tablespoons extra virgin olive oil
1 clove garlic, finely minced
1/2 cup coarsely chopped green olives stuffed with
    pimentos

Romano or Parmesan cheese, freshly grated, for
    topping

Make the pasta: Place the flour in a large mixing
bowl. Make a deep well in the center of the flour.
Carefully break the eggs into the well. Sprinkle the
salt on top of the eggs. With a fork, begin to move
in a circular motion around in the eggs. As bits of
flour begin to blend into the eggs, move the fork in a
larger circle. Continue blending until the fork no
longer moves freely.

With your hands, work the dough into a ball,
working in as much flour as possible. (Some bits
may separate and resist incorporation. Work them
in if possible; if not, discard them.) The ball will not
be smooth but will tend to separate. Using the flour
remaining in the bowl (about 1/4 cup) liberally dust
your rolling surface. With your hands, kneed the
ball as if kneeding bread, pressing away from you

with the heel of your hand, folding over the dough, turning it a quarter turn and repeating the process. Kneed about 10 minutes, or until the dough can be formed into a smooth ball. Cover the ball with a clean, dry kitchen towel and let rest at least 30 minutes (2 hours is better). Sift any leftover flour to remove any unincorporated crumbs of pasta and reserve the flour for dusting your rolling surface.

During the last 30 minutes of the resting time, make the filling: Fold the spinach into a clean, dry towel or paper towel and press out as much moisture as possible. Heat a large skillet over moderately high heat and add the oil. When the oil is hot, add the onion and sauté, stirring occasionally, until lightly browned, about 3 minutes. Reduce heat to medium and add the garlic. Sauté 1 minute. Add the spinach and toss to coat with oil. Cook, stirring constantly, about 1 minute. Add the cheeses, basil and salt and pepper. Stir to heat thoroughly, about 3 minutes. Remove from heat and set aside.

Return to the pasta: If you have a pasta machine, prepare the pasta and feed it through to roll and stretch according to your machine's directions. If you are an experienced hand pasta maker, use your own technique to create a very thin, almost transparent rectangular sheet. If you are inexperienced at making pasta by hand (as we were when we first developed this recipe), begin by liberally dusting your rolling surface and rolling pin with flour. With your hand, flatten the ball of dough and form it into a roughly rectangular shape. (Maintaining a generally rectangular shape will help decrease waste and make assembling and cooking the ravioli much easier.) Roll, as if you were making a pie crust, from the center outward, giving the dough a quarter turn after each roll. If the dough sticks to the surface, loosen it with a dinner knife and dust the surface with flour.

When your dough is about 1/4" thick, begin to stretch it. Place the rolling pin at the edge furthest from you. Roll the pin toward you over the dough, pulling the edge of the dough over the pin. As you unroll away from you, simultaneously stretch the dough away from you and pull it outward along the pin with your hands. (If you have a partner in the kitchen, one of you can hold the dough in place while the other stretches it with the pin.) Give the dough a quarter turn after each stretch. When, at last, the dough is very thin and almost transparent, let it rest 1 minute before adding the filling.

Assemble the ravioli: Bring a large pot of water to a boil and add 1 tablespoon olive oil. Cut your pasta sheet into 2 rectangles of equal size. Place the spinach filling in little mounds of about $1^1/2$ teaspoon each, carefully aligned and regimented, about 2" apart on one sheet. Keep the areas between the mounds perfectly clean and dry. Lay the second sheet on top of the first, carefully aligning the edges. With a ravioli cutter, a pizza cutter or even a very sharp knife, carefully slice between the mounds, separating the sheets into 2" squares. If using a pizza cutter or knife, seal the edges of each square by pressing them firmly with the tynes of a dinner fork. If the edges are not completely sealed, use a tiny bit of water and press with the fork. Work quickly to prevent the pasta from drying out.

Gently drop the ravioli squares into the boiling water, in batches if necessary (do not crowd the pot!), and cook for about 2 minutes.

While the ravioli cooks, make the sauce: Heat a small skillet over moderately high heat and add the oil. When the oil is hot, add the garlic and olives and sauté, stirring frequently, about 2-3 minutes. Lower the heat, if necessary, to prevent the garlic from browning.

Drain the ravioli thoroughly in a colander and immediately arrange on a warm serving platter or on individual plates. Drizzle the sauce over the ravioli and top with the grated cheese. Serve with crusty Italian bread.

GRANDMOTHER'S MEATBALLS

For a party of 6-8.
Preparation time: about 45 minutes.

1 pound lean ground beef
1/2 pound lean ground pork
1 pound ground white meat of turkey
1 egg white
1 teaspoon Worcestershire sauce
1/4 cup finely minced Italian parsley
1 tablespoon instant chopped onion
1 teaspoon ground basil
1 teaspoon ground oregano

1/4 cup very finely crushed bread crumbs
Salt and freshly ground black pepper, to taste
2 tablespoons (or more) extra virgin olive oil
Romano or Parmesan cheese, freshly grated, for
    topping

In a large bowl, combine the beef, pork and turkey and mix well. Add the egg white, Worcestershire sauce, parsley, onion, basil, oregano, bread crumbs and salt and pepper. Using your hands, mix the ingredients together until all are thoroughly combined. With wet hands, form the mixture into firm balls, about 1^1/2" in diameter.

Heat a large skillet over medium-low heat and add the olive oil. When the oil is hot, add the meatballs, in batches if necessary, and cook, turning frequently and adding more oil as needed, until the meatballs are evenly browned outside and cooked through, about 30 minutes. Remove the meatballs from the oil and drain on paper towels. Sprinkle the meatballs with the cheese and serve immediately.

THAT CHAMPIONSHIP SEASON
By Jason Miller
(1972)

Five men and their former coach meet annually to celebrate the 1952 Pennsylvania High School Basketball season. Only this triumph of their youth holds them together; otherwise, the gathering is a bitter and sad occasion, as they attack each other with the energy and determination that once made them a team.

From the beginning, it is a drinking celebration during which just about everything is out of control, including the chicken. "Chicken's in the oven," says Phil in Act I. Later George announces that the "chicken is in the stove." By the end of Act II, the chicken is nearly burned. With unrepentant irony, we offer the following recipe.

CHICKEN OF CHAMPIONS

For a party of 4.
Preparation time: about 1 hour, including baking.

3 tablespoons melted butter or margarine
A 2 $1/2$-3 pound chicken, cut into serving pieces
2-3 medium baking potatoes, scrubbed and cut into
      $1^1/2$" chunks
1 teaspoon dried parsley
1 teaspoon season salt

Juice of 2 limes
2 medium onions, peeled and cut into wedges
Freshly ground black pepper, to taste

Preheat the oven to 400° F.

With 1 tablespoon of the butter or margarine, grease a large baking dish.

In a large bowl, toss the chicken and potatoes to coat with the remaining butter or margarine. Place the chicken and potatoes in a single layer in the baking dish and sprinkle with the parsley and season salt. Add the onions to the dish; drizzle all with 1 tablespoon of the lime juice and sprinkle with the pepper.

Loosely cover the pan with foil and bake in the middle of the oven 30 minutes. Remove the foil, turn the chicken over and bake 15 minutes more.

Before serving, sprinkle with the remaining lime juice and brush with the pan juices.

⊕ ⊕ ⊕ ⊕ ⊕

As the men reminisce in Act II, the Coach refers to his unmarried state. But he has his memories:

> Miss Morris, remember her, the music teacher. We knew each other for years. Biblically. Used to visit her on Saturday afternoon. She'd make me honey bisquits. A very cultured woman . . .

MISS MORRIS' HONEY BISQUITS

For a party of 4-6 (Makes 12 bisquits).
Preparation time: about 30 minutes.

3 cups unbleached flour
4 $1/2$ teaspoons baking powder
1/2 teaspoon (or less) salt
1/2 cup vegetable shortening
1/4 cup honey
1/2 cup non-fat plain yoghurt
1/2 cup plus 1 tablespoon milk

Preheat the oven to 400° F.

In a large bowl, combine the flour, baking powder
and salt and mix well. Blend in the shortening with
a dough blender. Add the honey and work it into
the flour mixture with a fork. Add the yoghurt and
1/2 cup milk and continue working with a fork and
your hands until the mixture becomes a workable
dough. Hand form the dough into 12 equal bisquits
and place on a greased baking sheet. Brush the top
of each bisquit with the remaining milk. Bake in the
middle of the oven until golden, about 12-15
minutes.

Serve hot, with butter or margarine and honey or
marmalade.

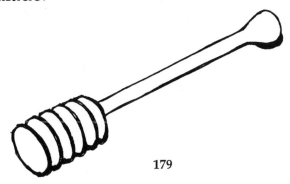

179

THIS MUSIC CREPT BY ME
UPON THE WATERS
By Archibald MacLeish
(1953)

A celebrated poet before World War II, MacLeish wrote radio plays during the 1930's and, after the War, began to write for the theatre. He favored what he called the "word-excited imagination," which becomes clear in *This Music Crept By Me Upon the Waters.* Two sophisticated people believe that they have found happiness and fulfillment on an island in the Antilles, where they are escaping the socially acceptable barbarians.

In this piece MacLeish is more interested in creating mood and character than dramatic action. At a dinner party, the moon entrances the guests.

As the hostess explains their evening meal:
> Island chickens
> Cook forever without noticing;
> All you need to do is baste them.
> Island diners baste themselves.

There will be bread, we are told, and we suggest a dish of Caribbean Rice to accompany the Island Chickens.

ISLAND CHICKENS

For a party of 4-8, depending upon appetites and
the size of the birds.

Preparation time: about 1 hour and 15 minutes,
including roasting.

4 Cornish hens, pigeons, guinea fowl or squabs
2 teaspoons dried rosemary
2 teaspoons dry mustard
1/2 teaspoon freshly ground black pepper
4 tablespoons butter or margarine
4 tablespoons flour
4 cloves garlic, peeled and quartered lengthwise

For the glaze:
1 tablespoon butter or margarine
1/4 cup ginger conserve
1/3 cup pineapple preserves
2 tablespoons fresh lemon juice
1/4 cup vinegar
1 tablespoon cornstarch
1/8 teaspoon (or less) salt

1 orange, cut into wedges, for garnish

Preheat the oven to 450° F.

Wash the birds, inside and out, with cold water.
Blot dry with paper towels. Mix the rosemary,
mustard and black pepper and sprinkle 2 teaspoons
of the mixture into the cavities of the birds. Place 4
pieces of garlic in each cavity. Truss the birds for
roasting (neck and lower cavities closed with
skewers, wings and legs tied closely to the body).

In a small bowl, blend the butter or margarine and the flour to make a smooth paste (roux). Blend the remaining spice mixture into the roux and spread the mixture evenly over the breasts, legs and wings. Arrange the birds in a large, well greased baking dish and place in the middle of the oven. Immediately reduce heat to 350° F.

Make the glaze: In a small saucepan, melt the butter or margarine over medium heat. Add the conserve, preserves and lemon juice. Cook, stirring frequently, until bubbly. Add the vinegar, cornstarch and salt. Cook, stirring constantly, until thickened.

When the birds have cooked 30 minutes, baste with the glaze and bake 15 minutes more. Baste again and cook another 15 minutes. Remove the birds from the oven and let stand about 10 minutes.

While the Island Chickens are very impressive served whole, we find half a bird plenty for one person. If your guests, too, have smaller appetites, split each bird in half, lengthwise. Garnish with the orange wedges and serve with Caribbean rice.

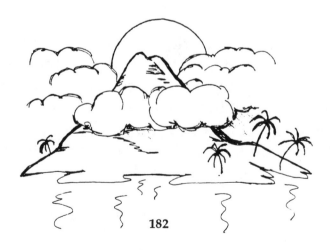

CARIBBEAN RICE

For a party of 6.
Preparation time: about 40 minutes, including simmering.

2-3 sprigs fresh cilantro, chopped
1 sprig fresh parsley, chopped
2 cloves garlic, peeled and minced
1/4 teaspoon freshly ground black pepper
3 scallions, chopped (green and white parts)
1 teaspoon cumin seed, toasted and ground
1/2 teaspoon coriander seed, toasted and ground
2 tablespoons canola oil or safflour oil
2 cups white rice
4 cups chicken stock
1 bay leaf
1 small canned jalapeño pepper, minced
1 ripe avocado, for garnish

In a mortar, pound the cilantro, parsley, garlic, black pepper, scallions, cumin and coriander into a paste. Set aside.

Heat the oil in a large saucepan over medium heat and stir in the rice. Cook, stirring constantly, about 2 minutes. Stir in the paste and stock. Raise heat to high and bring to a boil. Immediately reduce heat to simmer and add the bay leaf and jalapeño pepper. Cover tightly and cook 20 minutes. Remove from heat and let stand, covered, about 5 minutes. If any liquid remains, return the pan to low heat and simmer, stirring constantly, until the liquid evaporates. Remove and discard the bay leaf. Slice the avocado and serve with the hot rice.

THE THREE PENNY OPERA
By Bertolt Brecht and Kurt Weill
(1928)

Brecht achieved his first real success with this entertaining reworking of John Gay's *Beggar's Opera*. Presumably, Brecht meant to denounce the hypocrisy of the lower class and ridicule the middle class through his use of whores and thieves. But the vitality of the music and characters generally overwhelms the didactic quality of the play.

In the Soho district of London, Act I, Scene 2, MacHeath prepares to celebrate his marriage to Polly Peachum, daughter of the King of Beggars. They and their ragamuffin guests sit down to the wedding breakfast.

> Ed (pointing to the service): Lovely plates, Savoy Hotel.
> Jacob: The eggs mayonnaise are from Selfridge's. We had a jar of goose liver, too. But Jimmy ate it out of spite. He said he had an empty belly.

THREE PENNY EGGS MAYONNAISE

For a party of 6-8.
Preparation time: about 3 hours, including chilling.

6-8 eggs

For the mayonnaise:
2 large egg yolks, at room temperature
2 teaspoons wine vinegar
1 teaspoon Dijon mustard
A pinch salt
1/8 teaspoon freshly ground white pepper
$1^1/2$ cups extra virgin olive oil
2-3 teaspoons fresh lemon juice
Light cream, for thinning

For the garnish:
6-8 whole leaves red or green leaf lettuce
Freshly ground black pepper, to taste
Paprika, to taste
3-4 tablespoons chopped pimento
6-8 sprigs fresh parsley

Fill a large saucepan with water and bring it to a full, rolling boil. Carefully drop the eggs into the water and boil about 15 minutes. Drain the eggs and allow to cool slightly. Chill in the refrigerator.

Make the mayonnaise: In a warm medium mixing bowl, combine the egg yolks, 1 teaspoon of the vinegar, the mustard, salt and white pepper. With an electric mixer on high speed, beat until thoroughly blended.

One drop at a time, add 1/2 cup of the oil, beating constantly. Add the remaining vinegar and the remaining oil in a stream, beating constantly. Add the lemon juice, and more salt and pepper, if desired. If the mayonnaise is too thick, blend in enough cream to reach the desired consistency.

Remove the eggs from the refrigerator, peel and discard the eggshells. Serve the eggs halved, quartered or sliced on a bed of green or red leaf lettuce. Spoon the mayonnaise over the eggs, sprinkle with the black pepper and paprika and garnish with the slices of pimento and sprigs of fresh parsley.

⚓ ⚓ ⚓ ⚓ ⚓

As the guests discuss the meal, MacHeath berates Crookfinger Jacob about the knife in his hand and the trout in his plate.

> MacHeath: Have you ever seen such a thing, Polly? Eating fish with a knife! A person who does that is a pig, you understand, Jacob? You'll have a lot to do, Polly, before you can teach these oafs to behave like men.

Complete place settings should be on the dining table and used properly for complete satisfaction in eating the following preparation.

PANFRIED BROOK TROUT

For a party of 4.
Preparation time: about 15 minutes.

1 pound new potatoes, cut into $1^1/2$" cubes
4 whole trout, about 10 ounces each, cleaned
8 sprigs fresh thyme
1/4 cup butter or margarine

Salt and freshly ground black pepper, to taste
1 tablespoon minced fresh parsley or Italian parsley

Place the potatoes in a saucepan, cover with water, bring to a boil over high heat and cook until tender, about 15 minutes. Set aside.

Stuff each trout with 2 sprigs fresh thyme. Heat a large non-stick skillet over moderately high heat and add 1/2 of the butter or margarine. When melted and bubbly, add 2 trout. Cook, turning once, until the trout is opaque near the bone, about 5-6 minutes. Season with salt and pepper. Remove the trout from the skillet and keep warm. Repeat the process with the remaining butter or margarine and the other two trout. Add the potatoes to the skillet and cook until lightly browned.

Arrange the trout and potatoes on a warm serving platter or individual plates and sprinkle with the minced parsely.

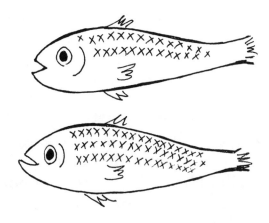

THE TIME OF YOUR LIFE
By William Saroyan
(1939)

In modern American drama, Saroyan's plays represent that healthy fantasy world that everyone should enter once in a while -- but with caution. "I seem to insist that people are good," he once wrote, "that living is good, that decency is right, that good is not only achievable but irresistible -- and there does not appear to be any justification for this."

The scene is Nick's Pacific Street Restaurant, Saloon and Entertainment Palace, a waterfront honky-tonk in San Francisco. The central character is Joe, a man who would rather believe in dreams than statistics, a poet-philosopher, a helper of the common man. Around him revolves a world of vaudeville and melodrama. "In the time of your life," Joe says, "Live -- so that in that good time there shall be no ugliness or death for yourself or for any life your life touches. Seek goodness every-where. . . ."

Joe helps Tom and Kitty, two of Saroyan's "beautiful people," incapable of dealing successfully with the world around them. Joe supports their dream: "Talk to her, Tom. Be the wonderful doctor she dreamed about and never found. Go ahead. Correct the errors of the world."

188

In Act I Joe has already helped Tom in a very real way.

> Joe: Who saved your life?
> Tom: You did, Joe. Thanks.
> Joe: How'd I do it? . . . I want you to answer me . . . I've forgotten.
> Tom: You made me eat all that chicken soup three years ago when I was sick and hungry.

JOE'S CHICKEN SOUP

For a party of 6-8.
Preparation time: about 3 hours, including simmering.

1 whole chicken, about 3 pounds, cut into pieces
1 medium onion, quartered
1 carrot, cut into 3-4 pieces
1 rib celery with leaves, cut into 3-4 pieces
1 bay leaf
8-10 whole black peppercorns
2-3 sprigs fresh parsley
1/2 teaspoon dried thyme
8 ounces uncooked noodles

In a large pot, bring 2 $1/2$ quarts of water to a full boil. Add the chicken and return to a boil, skimming off foam as it forms on the top.

Add the onion, carrot, celery, bay leaf, peppercorns, parsley and thyme. Reduce heat, cover and simmer about $1^1/2$ hours, or until the chicken falls off the bone when touched gently with a knife or fork.

189

While the chicken simmers, cook the noodles *al dente*, according to package directions. Drain and set aside.

Remove the chicken from the pot and set aside. Drain the stock and discard the vegetables and other solids. Skim off the fat (or refrigerate the stock, uncovered, overnight, then lift off and discard the fat layer which has formed on top).

Return the stock to the pot. Remove the skin and bones from the chicken. Dice about 2 $1/2$ cups of the chicken, reserving the remainder for another use. Add the diced chicken to the pot and heat to simmer. Do not allow the soup to boil!

Add the noodles and cook just long enough to heat through. Remove the soup from heat and pour into a heated tureen. Serve in heated bowls with crusty bread or crisp crackers.

THE WILD DUCK
By Henrik Ibsen
(1884)

Historians of the drama date the beginnings of modern drama with the mid-nineteenth century early plays of Ibsen. *The Wild Duck* is a transitional piece, a play that Ibsen recognized as special, involving new methods and new beliefs. The play can be seen as a commentary on the shock of growing up when the "life-lie," as Dr. Relling describes it, is destroyed.

The scene in Act I is the study of the rich merchant, Werle, just off the dining room where Hialmar Ekdal will dine and then return to his much poorer circumstances at home. There, in Act II, Hialmar's young daughter Hedvig eagerly awaits his return and the tasty treat that he has promised to bring. But he brings no food -- only Werle's menu.

> Hedvig: Haven't you got anything else?
> Hialmar: I forgot the other things, I tell you. But you may take my word for it, these dainties are very unsatisfying. Sit down at the table and read the menu, and then I'll describe to you how the dishes taste.
> Hedvig (gulpling her tears): Thank you.

How sad for Hedvig -- and for us who know nothing of this fine dinner!

In Act III, however, Hialmar's wife Gina makes a herring salad. Dr. Relling and Molvik appear at the door as Hedvig brings in beer and brandy.

> Dr. Relling: Molvik got the idea he could smell herring salad, and then there was no holding him.

GINA'S *SILLSALAD* (HERRING SALAD)

For a party of 8 or more.
Preparation time: about $1^1/2$ hours, including chilling.

$1^2/3$ cup diced pickled herring
1/2 cup diced unpeeled red apple
3 tablespoons minced onion
2 medium potatoes, peeled, boiled and diced
A can (1 pound) diced beets, well drained
1/4 cup diced dill pickle
2 tablespoons sugar
2 tablespoons water
2 tablespoons white wine vinegar
Freshly ground black pepper, to taste
1/2 cup sour cream or non-fat sour cream substitute
Sprigs of fresh parsley, for garnish

In a large bowl, combine the herring, apple, onion, beets and pickle. In another bowl, mix the sugar, water, vinegar and pepper and add to the herring mixture. Fold in the sour cream and blend gently. Refrigerate for 1 hour or more.

Drain off the liquid, if necessary. Garnish with the fresh parsley.

INDEX TO AUTHORS

INDEX TO RECIPES

- Notes -